Object Lifetime Puzzlers Book 3

128 Fun Puzzles

Jason Turner

Object Lifetime Puzzlers Book 3

128 Fun Puzzles

Jason Turner

ISBN 9798817265606

Also By Jason Turner

C++ Best Practices

Object Lifetime Puzzlers Book 1

Copy and Reference Puzzlers Book 1

Opcode Puzzlers Book 1

Object Lifetime Puzzlers Book 2

Copy and Reference Puzzlers Book 2

Copy and Reference Puzzlers Book 3

The Land Of Objects

Welcome to the land of objects. In this land, objects say their first name when their lifetime begins, and say their last name when their lifetime ends.

We have four different types of object lifetimes that we will eventually encounter.

- automatic
- static
- thread_local
- dynamic

Each type of lifetime has its own rules for when the lifetime begins and lifetime ends, and we'll explain them as we get to them!

Object Declaration

Every object in our land looks like this:

Basic Object Declaration

```
S object_1("First Name", "Last Name");
```

- `S`: The object's Type
- `object_1`: The object's ID
- `"First Name"`: The object's first name
- `"Last Name"`: The object's last name

Important note:

Anything starting with // is a "comment" and has no impact on the code!

A Note On Puzzle Layout

Some puzzles split across pages. Sometimes this is annoying. I've decided to leave it how it is because it adds a sense of realism to what it's actually like to read unnecessarily complex C++ code.

How C++ Relates

Each of these examples are real C++ code. If you are a C++ user, you can learn more about object lifetime with these puzzles.

These puzzles come directly from classes that I teach with C++ programmers. If you find them interesting, contact me about training. https://articles.emptycrate.com/training.html

Each solution is a topic that has something to do with C++. If you cannot figure out what the solution means, then duckduckgo for it and learn something new :).

If you aren't a C++ user then don't worry about any of this, just have fun!

Automatic Lifetime

Automatic lifetime is the default. Objects with automatic lifetime have their lifetime begin when their ID is first seen, and their lifetime end when their ID is no longer visible (after the ending }).

Automatic Object Example 1

```
void run() {
  S object_1("1", "2");
}
```

When this code is run, this is what happens:

Automatic Object Example 1 Results

```
void run() {
  S object_1("1", "2");  // 1 is printed
}                        // 2 is printed, object_1 is no longer visible
```

The output is:

Automatic Object Example 1 Output

```
12
```

Objects' lifetimes end in the reverse order they begin:

Automatic Object Example 2

```
void run() {
  S object_1("1", "2");
  S object_2("3", "4");
}
```

When this code is run, this is what happens:

Automatic Object Example 2 Results

```
void run() {
  S object_1("1", "2");  // 1 is printed
  S object_2("3", "4");  // 3 is printed
} // 4 is printed, object_2's lifetime ends first
  // 2 is printed, object_1's lifetime ends second
```

The output is:

Automatic Object Example 2 Output

```
1342
```

We can introduce a new "scope" with a `{`. Now remember, an "automatic" object's lifetime ends when its ID is no longer visible. When it "goes out of scope."

Automatic Object Example Scopes

```
void run() {
  {
    S object_1("1", "2");
  }
  S object_2("3", "4");
}
```

When this code is run, this is what happens:

Automatic Object Example Scopes Results

```
void run() {
  {
    S object_1("1", "2"); // 1
  }                       // 2
  S object_2("3", "4");   // 3
}                         // 4
```

The output is:

Automatic Object Example Scopes Output

```
1234
```

Automatic Lifetime Puzzles

Puzzle 1

```
void run() {
  S object_1("a", "n");
  S object_2("s", "i");
}

// Answer (4):

// __ __ __ __
```

Puzzle 2

```
void run() {
  {
    S object_1("e", "t");
    {
      S object_2("x", "t");
    }
    S object_3("e", "n");
  }
}

// Answer (6):

// __ __ __ __ __ __
```

Puzzle 3

```
void run() {
  S object_1("p", "t");
  {
    S object_2("o", "n");
    {
      S object_3("p", "c");
    }
    S object_4("o", "u");
  }
```

```
}

// Answer (8):

// __ __ __ __ __ __ __ __
```

Puzzle 4

```
void run() {
  {
    {
      S object_1("t", "c");
      {
        S object_2("e", "m");
      }
      S object_3("p", ".");
    }
    S object_4("l", "a");
  }
  S object_5("s", "s");
}

// Answer (10):

// __ __ __ __ __ __ __ __ __ __
```

Puzzle 5

```
void run() {
  {
    S object_1("r", "a");
  }
  {
    S object_2("n", "g");
  }
  S object_3("e", "f");
  {
    S object_4("s", ":");
  }
  S object_5(":", "o");
  S object_6("a", "_");
  S object_7("n", "y");
}
```

```
// Answer (14):

// __ __ __ __ __ __ __ __ __ __ __ __ __ __
```

Puzzle 6

```
void run() {
  {
    {
      S object_1("c", "c");
      {
        S object_2("o", "t");
        {
          S object_3("n", "c");
        }
        S object_4("e", "p");
      }
      S object_5("s", ".");
    }
    S object_6("o", "m");
  }
  S object_7("p", "e");
  S object_8("a", "r");
}

// Answer (16):

// __ __ __ __ __ __ __ __ __ __ __ __ __ __ __ __
```

Puzzle 7

```
void run() {
  {
    S object_1("c", "u");
    {
      S object_2("o", "p");
    }
    {
      S object_3("y", "s");
      {
        S object_4("_", "c");
      }
```

```
      S object_5("o", "n");
    }
    S object_6("t", "r");
  }
  S object_7("c", "e");
  S object_8("t", "l");
  S object_9("i", "b");
}

// Answer (18):

// __ __ __ __ __ __ __ __ __ __ __ __ __ __ __ __ __ __
```

Puzzle 8

```
void run() {
  {
    S object_1("t", "h");
  }
  {
    S object_2("r", ".");
    {
      S object_3("e", "a");
    }
    {
      S object_4("d", "e");
      {
        S object_5(".", "t");
      }
      S object_6("h", "r");
    }
    S object_7("a", "d");
  }
  S object_8("s", "c");
  S object_9("t", "i");
  S object_10("a", "t");
}

// Answer (20):

// __ __ __ __ __ __ __ __ __ __ __ __ __ __ __ __ __ __ __ __
```

Missing Objects

Sometimes objects (or operations) will be missing. It is your job to fill in the missing operation.

Missing Object Example Puzzle

```
void run() {
  {
    /* __________ */
  }
  S object_2("o", "t");
}

Answer (4):

woot
```

You need to fill in the blank with the missing operation that completes the puzzle.

Missing Object Example Solution

```
void run() {
  {
    /* __________ */ S object_1("w", "o");
  }
  S object_2("o", "t");
}

Answer (4):

woot
```

Missing Object Puzzles

Puzzle 9

```
void run() {
  {
    /* ________ */
  }
  S object_2("v", "e");
}

// Answer (4):

// move
```

Puzzle 10

```
void run() {
  {
    {
      S object_1("g", "r");
    }
    S object_2("a", "m");
  }
  S object_3(".", "s");
  S object_4("c", "s");
  /* ________ */
}

// Answer (10):

// gram.class
```

Puzzle 11

```
void run() {
  {
    /* ________ */
  }
  {
    S object_2("s", "b");
    {
      S object_3("_", "l");
      {
        S object_4("s", "i");
      }
      S object_5("n", "g");
    }
    S object_6("e", "_");
  }
  S object_7("i", "t");
}

// Answer (14):

// has_single_bit
```

Puzzle 12

```
void run() {
  {
    {
      S object_1("r", "g");
      {
        S object_2("a", "n");
      }
      S object_3("g", ".");
      {
        /* ________ */
        {
          S object_5(".", "a");
        }
        S object_6("c", "c");
      }
      S object_7("s", "s");
    }
```

```
    S object_8("e", "n");
  }
  S object_9("e", "l");
  S object_10("r", "a");
}

// Answer (20):

// range.access.general
```

Static Lifetime

Static objects, like automatic objects, have their lifetime begin the first time their ID is seen. Their lifetime ends not when they go out of scope, but instead when the program ends. **Objects' lifetimes still end in the reverse order they begin**:

static Example 1

```
void run() {
  static S object_1("1", "2");
  static S object_1("3", "4");
}
```

When this code is run, this is what happens:

static Example 1 Results

```
void run() {
  static S object_1("1", "2");  // 1 is printed
  static S object_2("3", "4");  // 3 is printed
}

// Program Ends

// 4 is printed, object_2's lifetime ends first
// 2 is printed, object_1's lifetime ends second
```

The output is:

static Example 1 Output

```
1342
```

Scopes do not impact static objects in the same way they impact automatic objects.

static Scopes Example

```
void run() {
  {
    static S object_1("1", "2");
  }
  static S object_2("3", "4");
}
```

When this code is run, this is what happens:

static Scopes Example Results

```
void run() {
  {
    static S object_1("1", "2"); // 1
  }
  static S object_2("3", "4");   // 3
}

// Program ends

// object_2's lifetime ends: 4
// object_1's lifetime ends: 2
```

The output is:

static Scopes Example Output

```
1342
```

Static Lifetime Puzzles

Puzzle 13

```
void run() {
  static S object_1("w", "f");
  {
    static S object_2("c", "o");
  }
  static S object_3("s", "t");
}

// Answer (6):

// __ __ __ __ __ __
```

Puzzle 14

```
void run() {
  {
    static S object_1("o", "b");
    {
      static S object_2("v", "u");
    }
    static S object_3("e", "s");
  }
  static S object_4("r", ".");
}

// Answer (8):

// __ __ __ __ __ __ __ __
```

Puzzle 15

```
void run() {
  {
    static S object_1("d", "t");
  }
  {
    static S object_2("y", "s");
  }
  static S object_3("n", "a");
  static S object_4("a", "c");
  static S object_5("m", "_");
  static S object_6("i", "c");
}

// Answer (12):

// __ __ __ __ __ __ __ __ __ __ __ __
```

Puzzle 16

```
void run() {
  static S object_1("s", "d");
  static S object_2("e", "e");
  {
    static S object_3("t", "t");
    {
      static S object_4("_", "c");
    }
    {
      static S object_5("u", "e");
    }
    static S object_6("n", "p");
  }
  static S object_7("e", "x");
}

// Answer (14):

// __ __ __ __ __ __ __ __ __ __ __ __ __ __
```

Puzzle 17

```
void run() {
  {
    static S object_1("f", "p");
  }
  {
    static S object_2("u", "a");
    {
      static S object_3("n", "c");
    }
    static S object_4("c", ".");
  }
  static S object_5(".", "c");
  static S object_6("w", "n");
  static S object_7("r", "u");
  static S object_8("a", "f");
  static S object_9("p", ".");
}

// Answer (18):

// __ __ __ __ __ __ __ __ __ __ __ __ __ __ __ __ __ __
```

Puzzle 18

```
void run() {
  {
    static S object_1("r", "w");
  }
  static S object_2("a", "e");
  {
    static S object_3("n", "i");
  }
  static S object_4("g", "v");
  {
    static S object_5("e", "r");
    {
      static S object_6(".", "e");
    }
    static S object_7("s", "v");
  }
  static S object_8("p", "o");
```

```
  static S object_9("l", ".");
  static S object_10("i", "t");
}

// Answer (20):

// __ __ __ __ __ __ __ __ __ __ __ __ __ __ __ __ __ __ __ __
```

Puzzle 19

```
void run() {
  {
    static S object_1("g", "f");
  }
  S object_2("e", "_");
  static S object_3("t", "i");
}

// Answer (6):

// __ __ __ __ __ __
```

Puzzle 20

```
void run() {
  {
    {
      S object_1("m", "b");
    }
    static S object_2("r", "6");
  }
  S object_3("t", "1");
  S object_4("o", "c");
}

// Answer (8):

// __ __ __ __ __ __ __ __
```

Puzzle 21

```
void run() {
  S object_1("m", "o");
  static S object_2("e", "r");
  {
    static S object_3("m", "e");
  }
  {
    static S object_4("o", "d");
    S object_5("r", "y");
  }
  static S object_6("_", "r");
}

// Answer (12):

// __ __ __ __ __ __ __ __ __ __ __ __
```

Puzzle 22

```
void run() {
  static S object_1("u", "p");
  S object_2("n", "i");
  {
    S object_3("o", "m");
    static S object_4("r", "a");
    S object_5("d", ".");
  }
  {
    static S object_6("u", "m");
    S object_7("l", "t");
  }
}

// Answer (14):

// __ __ __ __ __ __ __ __ __ __ __ __ __ __
```

Puzzle 23

```
void run() {
  {
    static S object_1("b", "t");
  }
  S object_2("a", "p");
  {
    S object_3("s", "o");
    {
      S object_4("i", "_");
      static S object_5("c", "m");
    }
    static S object_6("i", "f");
  }
  S object_7("s", "o");
  static S object_8(":", "y");
  S object_9(":", "c");
}

// Answer (18):

// __ __ __ __ __ __ __ __ __ __ __ __ __ __ __ __ __ __
```

Puzzle 24

```
void run() {
  {
    {
      S object_1("t", "i");
    }
    static S object_2("m", "s");
  }
  static S object_3("e", "r");
  {
    static S object_4(".", "e");
    {
      static S object_5("c", "b");
    }
    S object_6("a", "l");
  }
  S object_7(".", "m");
  static S object_8("y", "m");
```

```
  S object_9("m", ".");
  static S object_10("d", "e");
}

// Answer (20):

// __ __ __ __ __ __ __ __ __ __ __ __ __ __ __ __ __ __ __ __
```

Puzzle 25

```
void run() {
  {
    static S object_1("s", "h");
    S object_2("e", "a");
  }
  /* ________ */
}

// Answer (6):

// search
```

Puzzle 26

```
void run() {
  {
    /* ________ */
  }
  static S object_2("e", "c");
  S object_3("f", "o");
  {
    S object_4("e", "r");
  }
  S object_5("_", "l");
}

// Answer (10):

// defer_lock
```

Puzzle 27

```
void run() {
  /* ________ */
  {
    static S object_2("e", "n");
  }
  static S object_3("f", "o");
  {
    S object_4("n", "s");
  }
  {
    /* ________ */
  }
  S object_6("r", "c");
  static S object_7("o", "i");
  S object_8("j", "e");
}

// Answer (16):

// defns.projection
```

Puzzle 28

```
void run() {
  {
    static S object_1("d", "w");
    {
      /* ________ */
      {
        static S object_3("f", "o");
        {
          /* ________ */
          S object_5("s", ".");
        }
        static S object_6("a", "h");
      }
      S object_7("r", "u");
      static S object_8("g", "t");
    }
    S object_9("e", "n");
  }
```

```
  static S object_10("t", ".");
}

// Answer (20):

// defns.argument.throw
```

Formatting Does Not Matter

In C++ (the computer programming languages these puzzles are based on), formatting does not matter!

This example:

Formatting Doesn't Matter

```
void run() {
  {
    S object_1("1", "2");
  }
  S object_2("3", "4");
}
```

Produces exactly the same results as this example:

Formatting Doesn't Matter Example

```
void run() {
{ S object_1("1", "2"); } S object_2("3", "4");
}
```

This can make the puzzles much harder to read. Watch for this mixed-up formatting in the rest of this book.

Formatting Does Not Matter Puzzles

Puzzle 29

```
void run() {
{
  }
  S object_1("c", "r");
  S object_2("h", "a");
}

// Answer (4):

// __ __ __ __
```

Puzzle 30

```
void run() {
  S object_1("r", "p");
  S object_2("a", "o");
  S object_3("n", "r");
  {
    S object_4("g", "e");
  }
  {
    S object_5(".", "d");
  }
}

// Answer (10):

// __ __ __ __ __ __ __ __ __ __
```

Puzzle 31

```
void run() {
  S object_1("i", "e");
  S object_2("t", "g");
  S object_3("e", "n");
  S object_4("r", "a");
    {
  }
  S object_5("a", "r");
{
    {
      S object_6("t", "o");
    }
    {
      S object_7("r", ".");
    }
  }
}

// Answer (14):

// __ __ __ __ __ __ __ __ __ __ __ __ __ __
```

Puzzle 32

```
void run() {
  {
    S object_1("s", "t");
  }
  {
    S object_2("r", "n");
    {
      S object_3("i", ".");
        {
      }
      {
        S object_4("n", "g");
    }
      {
        S object_5("s", "t");
      }
      S object_6("r", "m");
```

```
        {
      }
      S object_7("e", "a");
    }
    S object_8("g", "e");
    }
    S object_9("e", "l");
  S object_10("r", "a");
}

// Answer (20):

// __ __ __ __ __ __ __ __ __ __ __ __ __ __ __ __ __ __ __ __
```

Dynamic Lifetime

Dynamic objects have their lifetimes begin when a `new` expression is executed, and their lifetimes end when a `delete` expression is executed.

Pointer Declaration

```
void run() {
  S *object_1 = nullptr;
}
```

The above example has 1 pointer and no `new` and no `delete`, so there's nothing to print!

Note: the astute among you will notice that there is still an object here. `object_1` is a trivial object with a type of `S *`.

Dynamic Objects Example

```
void run() {
  S *object_1 = new S("1", "2");
  delete S;
}
```

When this code is executed:

Dynamic Objects Example Results

```
void run() {
  S *object_1 = new S("1", "2"); // 1
  delete S;                      // 2
}
```

Dynamic objects can mess with our notion of when objects' lifetimes begin and end:

Dynamic Objects Deleted Out Of Order

```
void run() {
  S *object_1 = new S("1", "2"); // 1
  S *object_2 = new S("3", "4"); // 3
  delete object_1;               // 2
  delete object_2;               // 4
}
```

Dynamic Lifetime Puzzles

Puzzle 33

```
void run() {
  {
  }
  S *object_1 = new S("s", "e");
  delete object_1;
  S *object_2 = nullptr;
  S *object_3 = new S("t", "t");
}

// Answer (3):

// __ __ __
```

Puzzle 34

```
void run() {
  {
    S *object_1 = nullptr;
  }
  S *object_2 = new S("b", "i");
  S *object_3 = nullptr;
  delete object_2;
  object_3 = new S("t", "q");
  S *object_4 = nullptr;
}

// Answer (3):

// __ __ __
```

Puzzle 35

```
void run() {
  S *object_1 = nullptr;
  S *object_2 = new S("f", "o");
  {
    S *object_3 = new S("l", "x");
  }
  delete object_2;
  S *object_4 = nullptr;
  object_4 = new S("o", "r");
  S *object_5 = nullptr;
  delete object_4;
  {
    S *object_6 = new S("l", "h");
  }
}

// Answer (6):

// __ __ __ __ __ __
```

Puzzle 36

```
void run() {
  {
    S *object_1 = nullptr;
    {
    }
    object_1 = new S("g", "w");
  }
  {
  }
  S *object_2 = nullptr;
  object_2 = new S("r", "a");
  delete object_2;
  S *object_3 = nullptr;
  S *object_4 = new S("m", ".");
  S *object_5 = nullptr;
  delete object_4;
  S *object_6 = new S("b", "a");
  delete object_6;
  object_3 = new S("s", "x");
```

```
  object_5 = new S("i", "c");
  delete object_5;
  S *object_7 = nullptr;
}

// Answer (10):

// __ __ __ __ __ __ __ __ __ __
```

Puzzle 37

```
void run() {
  S *object_1 = nullptr;
  S *object_2 = new S("r", "w");
  object_1 = new S("a", "h");
  {
    S *object_3 = new S("n", "d");
  }
  S *object_4 = new S("g", "r");
  {
    S *object_5 = new S("e", ".");
    delete object_5;
  }
  S *object_6 = new S("s", "l");
  S *object_7 = nullptr;
  {
    S *object_8 = new S("p", "a");
  }
  delete object_6;
  object_7 = new S("i", "t");
  delete object_7;
  S *object_9 = nullptr;
}

// Answer (11):

// __ __ __ __ __ __ __ __ __ __ __
```

Puzzle 38

```
void run() {
  S *object_1 = nullptr;
  {
    {
      {
        S *object_2 = nullptr;
        object_2 = new S("r", "o");
        S *object_3 = nullptr;
      }
      object_1 = new S("e", "y");
      S *object_4 = new S("m", "k");
      S *object_5 = nullptr;
      S *object_6 = new S("q", "e");
      {
        object_5 = new S("u", "u");
        S *object_7 = nullptr;
        S *object_8 = new S("o", "x");
      }
      S *object_9 = new S("f", "y");
    }
    S *object_10 = nullptr;
  }
}

// Answer (7):

// __ __ __ __ __ __ __
```

Puzzle 39

```
void run() {
  {
    S *object_1 = nullptr;
  }
  S *object_2 = new S("t", "w");
  S *object_3 = new S("i", "p");
  S *object_4 = nullptr;
  object_4 = new S("m", "h");
  S object_5("e", "d");
}
```

```
// Answer (5):

// __ __ __ __ __
```

Puzzle 40

```
void run() {
  S *object_1 = nullptr;
  S *object_2 = new S("i", "s");
  S *object_3 = new S("o", "s");
  delete object_3;
  S object_4(".", "n");
  {
    S *object_5 = nullptr;
    delete object_2;
    {
      S *object_6 = new S("y", "d");
    }
  }
}

// Answer (7):

// __ __ __ __ __ __ __
```

Puzzle 41

```
void run() {
  S object_1("c", "t");
  S *object_2 = new S("m", "p");
  S *object_3 = nullptr;
  delete object_2;
  {
    object_3 = new S(".", "p");
  }
  S *object_4 = new S("c", "d");
  S *object_5 = new S("o", "e");
  S object_6("n", "p");
  {
    S object_7("c", "e");
  }
}
```

```
// Answer (11):

// __ __ __ __ __ __ __ __ __ __ __
```

Puzzle 42

```
void run() {
  S *object_1 = new S("s", "t");
  S object_2("t", "e");
  {
    S object_3("m", "i");
    {
      delete object_1;
      {
      }
    }
    S *object_4 = new S(".", "i");
    S object_5("w", "h");
  }
  S *object_6 = nullptr;
  S *object_7 = nullptr;
  S *object_8 = new S("l", "d");
}

// Answer (10):

// __ __ __ __ __ __ __ __ __ __
```

Puzzle 43

```
void run() {
  S *object_1 = new S("s", "i");
  S object_2("e", "w");
  S *object_3 = nullptr;
  {
    object_3 = new S("t", "v");
    S *object_4 = nullptr;
    S object_5(".", "o");
  }
  delete object_3;
  S *object_6 = new S("e", "i");
  S object_7("r", "e");
  {
```

```
    S *object_8 = nullptr;
    {
      S object_9("v", "i");
    }
  }
}

// Answer (12):

// __ __ __ __ __ __ __ __ __ __ __ __
```

Puzzle 44

```
void run() {
  S *object_1 = nullptr;
  {
    S object_2("r", "s");
    S *object_3 = new S("a", "g");
    object_1 = new S("n", "y");
    delete object_3;
    S *object_4 = new S("e", "p");
  }
  S *object_5 = new S(":", ":");
  {
    delete object_5;
    {
      S object_6("c", "g");
      S *object_7 = new S("r", "t");
      S object_8("b", "e");
    }
  }
  {
    S *object_9 = new S("i", "v");
  }
  S *object_10 = new S("n", "i");
}

// Answer (15):

// __ __ __ __ __ __ __ __ __ __ __ __ __ __ __
```

Puzzle 45

```
void run() {
  S *object_1 = new S("c", "o");
  {
    static S object_2("o", "e");
    S *object_3 = new S("r", "h");
  }
  delete object_1;
  static S object_4("u", "n");
  static S object_5("t", "i");
}

// Answer (9):

// __ __ __ __ __ __ __ __ __
```

Puzzle 46

```
void run() {
  S *object_1 = new S("r", "y");
  {
    static S object_2("a", "w");
  }
  {
    S *object_3 = new S("n", ".");
    static S object_4("g", "e");
    S *object_5 = new S("e", "s");
    delete object_3;
    static S object_6("v", "i");
  }
}

// Answer (10):

// __ __ __ __ __ __ __ __ __ __
```

Puzzle 47

```
void run() {
  static S object_1("o", "l"); S *object_2 = nullptr;
  static S object_3("p", "a");
  S *object_4 = new S("t", "f");
  {
    S *object_5 = nullptr;
    S *object_6 = new S("i", "l");
    static S object_7("o", "n");
  }
}

// Answer (8):

// __ __ __ __ __ __ __ __
```

Puzzle 48

```
void run() {
  static S object_1("s", "s");
  S *object_2 = nullptr;
  S *object_3 = new S("t", "r");
  {
    delete object_3;
  }
  S *object_4 = new S("i", "."); static S object_5("n", "p");
  S *object_6 = new S("g", "w");
  delete object_4;
  S *object_7 = nullptr;
  S *object_8 = new S("o", "p");
}

// Answer (10):

// __ __ __ __ __ __ __ __ __ __
```

Puzzle 49

```
void run() {
  S *object_1 = nullptr; object_1 = new S("i", "t");
  static S object_2("n", "r");
  {
    S *object_3 = new S("s", ".");
    {
      S *object_4 = nullptr;
      object_4 = new S("e", "a");
      static S object_5("r", "o");
      delete object_1;
      {
        delete object_3;
      }
      S *object_6 = nullptr;
      static S object_7("i", "t");
      object_6 = new S("t", "i");
      S *object_8 = new S("e", "r");
      static S object_9("r", "a");
    }
  }
}

// Answer (15):

// __ __ __ __ __ __ __ __ __ __ __ __ __ __ __
```

Puzzle 50

```
void run() {
  static S object_1("f", "n"); {
    {
      S *object_2 = nullptr;
    }
    S *object_3 = nullptr;
    S *object_4 = new S("u", "w");
  }
  {
    static S object_5("n", "f");
    static S object_6("c", "m");
    S *object_7 = nullptr; }
  {
```

```
    S *object_8 = new S(".", "n");
  }
  S *object_9 = nullptr;
  object_9 = new S("m", "w");
  S *object_10 = new S("e", "q");
}

// Answer (10):

// __ __ __ __ __ __ __ __ __ __
```

Puzzle 51

```
void run() {
S *object_1 = new S("f", "n");
  S *object_2 = new S("u", "i");
    delete object_1;
  {
    static S object_3("c", "f");
    S *object_4 = new S(".", "k");
    static S object_5("d", "e");
  }
}

// Answer (8):

// __ __ __ __ __ __ __ __
```

Puzzle 52

```
void run() {
  S *object_1 = nullptr;
  static S object_2("c", "g");
  S object_3("o", "i");
  {
    static S object_4("u", "n");
    S object_5("n", "t");
  }
  S *object_6 = nullptr;
}

// Answer (8):
```

```
// __ __ __ __ __ __ __ __
```

Puzzle 53

```
void run() {
  {
  }
  S *object_1 = new S("b", "i");
  delete object_1;
  S object_2("n", "r");
  S *object_3 = new S("a", "r");
  {
    delete object_3;
  }
  S object_4("y", "a");
    static S object_5("_", "h");
  S *object_6 = new S("s", "i");
  static S object_7("e", "c");
}

// Answer (13):

// __ __ __ __ __ __ __ __ __ __ __ __ __
```

Puzzle 54

```
void run() {
  S *object_1 = new S("s", "l");
  delete object_1;
S *object_2 = new S("i", "s");
  S object_3("c", "s");
  S *object_4 = new S("e", "r");
  {
    S *object_5 = nullptr;
  }
  S object_6(".", "e");
  S *object_7 = new S("a", "c");
  {
    delete object_7;
    {
      static S object_8("c", "s");
    }
```

```
  }
}

// Answer (12):

// __ __ __ __ __ __ __ __ __ __ __ __
```

Puzzle 55

```
void run() {
  {
    {
    }
    static S object_1("i", "e");
    S object_2("n", "d");
  }
  S *object_3 = new S("e", "_");
  {
    static S object_4("x", "c");
    }
  delete object_3;
  S *object_5 = nullptr;
  S *object_6 = new S("s", "e");
  object_5 = new S("e", "q");
  delete object_5;
  S object_7("u", "n");
  S *object_8 = nullptr;
  delete object_6;
  S *object_9 = nullptr;
}

// Answer (14):

// __ __ __ __ __ __ __ __ __ __ __ __ __ __
```

Puzzle 56

```
void run() {
  S *object_1 = new S("r", "i");
  S *object_2 = nullptr;
  object_2 = new S("e", "n");
  S object_3(".", "i");
  S *object_4 = nullptr;
  S object_5("r", "s");
  S *object_6 = new S("e", "o");
  static S object_7("s", "e");
  {
    S object_8("u", "t");
    static S object_9("l", "z");
  }
  S object_10("s", ".");
}

// Answer (15):

// __ __ __ __ __ __ __ __ __ __ __ __ __ __ __
```

Puzzle 57

```
void run() {
  S *object_1 = new S("r", "j");
  /* ________ */
  S *object_3 = new S(".", "n");
  S object_4("s", "y");
  {
    S *object_5 = nullptr;
  }
}

// Answer (6):

// re.syn
```

Puzzle 58

```
void run() {
  S *object_1 = nullptr;
  /* ________ */
  {
    delete object_2;
  }
  object_1 = new S("m", "m");
  S *object_3 = nullptr;
  S *object_4 = new S("q", "i");
  S object_5("u", "o");
}

// Answer (6):

// remquo
```

Puzzle 59

```
void run() {
  S object_1("e", "s");
  {
  }
  static S object_2("x", "t");
  S object_3("p", "n");
  S *object_4 = new S("r", "j");
  S *object_5 = new S(".", "u");
  /* ________ */
}

// Answer (10):

// expr.const
```

Puzzle 60

```
void run() {
  S *object_1 = new S("C", "o");
  delete object_1;
  S object_2("n", "n");
  static S object_3("t", "r");
  {
    /* ________ */
    {
      S *object_5 = nullptr;
      static S object_6("i", "e");
    }
  }
}

// Answer (9):

// Container
```

Puzzle 61

```
void run() {
  S *object_1 = nullptr;
  S *object_2 = new S("w", "x");
  object_1 = new S("m", "c");
  {
    S *object_3 = new S("e", "x");
  }
  S *object_4 = new S("m", "h");
  /* ________ */
  S *object_5 = nullptr;
  {
    /* ________ */
  }
}

// Answer (7):

// wmemchr
```

Puzzle 62

```
void run() {
  static S object_1("f", "t");
  {
    S *object_2 = new S("i", "a");
    static S object_3("n", "o");
    S object_4("d", "_");
    {
      /* ________ */
    }
    S *object_6 = new S("i", "i");
    /* ________ */
  }
}

// Answer (11):

// find_if_not
```

Puzzle 63

```
void run() {
  {
  }
  S *object_1 = nullptr;
  {
    S *object_2 = nullptr;
    /* ________ */
    object_1 = new S("u", "h");
    static S object_4("b", "t");
    S *object_5 = nullptr;
    static S object_6("t", "c");
  }
  /* ________ */
}

// Answer (8):

// subtract
```

Puzzle 64

```
void run() {
  S *object_1 = nullptr;
  {
    /* ________ */
    static S object_2("h", "q");
    S object_3("r", ".");
    {
      S *object_4 = nullptr;
      /* ________ */
      S *object_6 = new S("a", "s");
    }
    static S object_7("d", "r");
  }
}

// Answer (10):

// thread.req
```

Puzzle 65

```
void run() {
  static S object_1("d", "t");
  S object_2("c", "i");
  {
    S *object_3 = nullptr;
    {
      static S object_4("l", "i");
      object_3 = new S(".", "e");
      S *object_5 = new S("c", "n");
      S *object_6 = nullptr;
      {
        /* ________ */
        delete object_5;
        object_6 = new S("s", "e");
        /* ________ */
      }
    }
  }
}
```

```
// Answer (13):

// dcl.constinit
```

Puzzle 66

```
void run() {
  S *object_1 = nullptr;
  {
    /* ________ */
  }
  static S object_3("s", "t");
  /* ________ */
  {
    object_1 = new S("b", "s");
    S object_5("a", "n");
    delete object_1;
    {
      S *object_6 = nullptr;
      S *object_7 = new S("e", ":");
      delete object_7;
      object_6 = new S(":", "x");
      S *object_8 = new S("I", "k");
    }
  }
}

// Answer (14):

// ios_base::Init
```

Puzzle 67

```
void run() {
  S object_1("i", "t");
  /* ________ */
  S *object_3 = nullptr;
  /* ________ */
  S *object_5 = new S("p", "l");
  delete object_5;
  S *object_6 = new S("a", "g");
  static S object_7("c", "y");
  S object_8("e", "_");
```

```
}

// Answer (13):

// in_place_type
```

Puzzle 68

```
void run() {
  static S object_1("t", "o");
  S *object_2 = nullptr;
  object_2 = new S("i", "r");
  S *object_3 = nullptr;
  S object_4("m", "n");
  static S object_5("e", "i");
  S *object_6 = new S(".", "u");
  S object_7("d", "o");
  {
    /* ________ */
  }
  delete object_2;
  static S object_8("a", ".");
  /* ________ */
}

// Answer (16):

// time.duration.io
```

Puzzle 69

```
void run() {
  S object_1("r", "e");
  {
    /* ________ */
  }
  S *object_3 = nullptr;
  {
    /* ________ */
    {
      S object_5("e", "s");
    }
    object_3 = new S(":", "s");
```

```
    /* ________ */
    S *object_7 = nullptr;
  }
  S *object_8 = new S("r", "b");
  S *object_9 = new S("g", "o");
}

// Answer (13):

// ranges::merge
```

Puzzle 70

```
void run() {
  static S object_1("t", "l");
  S *object_2 = nullptr;
  /* ________ */
  /* ________ */
  S object_4("e", "e");
  S *object_5 = new S(".", "t");
  S object_6("c", "n");
  {
    static S object_7("a", "a");
    S object_8("l", "e");
    delete object_2;
    /* ________ */
  }
}

// Answer (16):

// time.cal.general
```

Puzzle 71

```
void run() {
  {
    S object_1("c", "i");
    static S object_2("s", "l");
    S object_3("t", "d");
  }
  S *object_4 = nullptr;
  /* ________ */
  {
    /* ________ */
    {
      static S object_7(".", "a");
      {
        /* ________ */
        static S object_8("e", "r");
        S *object_9 = nullptr;
        static S object_10("n", "e");
      }
    }
  }
}

// Answer (15):

// cstdint.general
```

Puzzle 72

```
void run() {
  {
    S *object_1 = new S("r", "r");
    static S object_2("a", "a");
  }
  S *object_3 = nullptr;
  static S object_4("n", "t");
  S *object_5 = new S("g", "i");
  /* ________ */
  {
    S *object_6 = nullptr;
    delete object_3;
  }
```

```
  S *object_7 = nullptr;
  /* ________ */
  S object_9("r", "d");
  /* ________ */
  object_7 = new S("m", "a");
  S object_10(".", "c");
}

// Answer (16):

// range.prim.cdata
```

Thread Local Lifetime

`thread_local` is very similar to `static`, with one very important difference: their lifetimes end not when the program ends, but when the thread ends! If you don't know what a thread is, don't worry about it. The important thing to know is that the thread ends before the program ends.

thread_local Example

```
void run() {
  {
    thread_local S object_1("1", "2");
  }
  thread_local S object_2("3", "4");
}
```

When this code is run, this is what happens:

thread_local Example Results

```
void run() {
  {
    thread_local S object_1("1", "2"); // 1
  }
  thread_local S object_2("3", "4");   // 3
}

// Thread Ends

// object_2's lifetime ends: 4
// object_1's lifetime ends: 2

// Program Ends

// Nothing to print here!
```

The output is:

thread_local Example Output

```
1342
```

Keeping in mind what happens first is going to be very key to solving puzzles with both `thread_local` and `static` objects in them!

Thread Local Lifetime Puzzles

Puzzle 73

```
void run() {
  {
    thread_local S object_1("r", "n");
  }
  thread_local S object_2("a", "i");
  thread_local S object_3("n", ":");
  thread_local S object_4("g", ":");
  thread_local S object_5("e", "s");
}

// Answer (10):

// __ __ __ __ __ __ __ __ __ __
```

Puzzle 74

```
void run() {
  {
    thread_local S object_1("b", "g");
    {
      thread_local S object_2("a", "n");
    }
    thread_local S object_3("s", "i");
  }
  thread_local S object_4("i", "r");
  thread_local S object_5("c", "t");
  thread_local S object_6("_", "s");
}

// Answer (12):

// __ __ __ __ __ __ __ __ __ __ __ __
```

Puzzle 75

```
void run() {
  {
    thread_local S object_1("r", "n");
    {
      thread_local S object_2("a", "_");
    }
    thread_local S object_3("n", "l");
  }
  thread_local S object_4("g", "l");
  thread_local S object_5("e", "i");
  thread_local S object_6("s", "f");
  thread_local S object_7(":", ":");
}

// Answer (14):

// __ __ __ __ __ __ __ __ __ __ __ __ __ __
```

Puzzle 76

```
void run() {
  {
    thread_local S object_1("s", "y");
  }
  {
    thread_local S object_2("t", "r");
    {
      thread_local S object_3("a", "t");
    }
    thread_local S object_4("c", "n");
  }
  thread_local S object_5("k", "e");
  thread_local S object_6("t", ".");
  thread_local S object_7("r", "e");
  thread_local S object_8("a", "c");
}

// Answer (16):

// __ __ __ __ __ __ __ __ __ __ __ __ __ __ __ __
```

Puzzle 77

```
void run() {
  thread_local S object_1("c", "t");
  {
    thread_local S object_2("o", "_");
  }
  {
    thread_local S object_3("m", "e");
  }
  thread_local S object_4("m", "c");
  {
    thread_local S object_5("o", "n");
  }
  thread_local S object_6("n", "e");
  thread_local S object_7("_", "r");
  thread_local S object_8("r", "e");
  thread_local S object_9("e", "f");
}

// Answer (18):

// __ __ __ __ __ __ __ __ __ __ __ __ __ __ __ __ __ __
```

Puzzle 78

```
void run() {
  thread_local S object_1("s", "s");
  {
    thread_local S object_2("t", "b");
  }
  {
    thread_local S object_3("a", "o");
  }
  thread_local S object_4("c", ".");
  {
    thread_local S object_5("k", "c");
    {
      thread_local S object_6("t", "i");
    }
    thread_local S object_7("r", "s");
  }
  thread_local S object_8("a", "a");
```

```
  thread_local S object_9("c", "b");
  thread_local S object_10("e", ".");
}

// Answer (20):

// __ __ __ __ __ __ __ __ __ __ __ __ __ __ __ __ __ __ __ __
```

Puzzle 79

```
void run() {
  thread_local S object_1("t", "o");
  static S object_2("i", "t");
  {
    static S object_3("m", "n");
  }
  static S object_4("e", "i");
  thread_local S object_5(".", "p");
}

// Answer (10):

// __ __ __ __ __ __ __ __ __ __
```

Puzzle 80

```
void run() {
  {
    thread_local S object_1("f", "u");
  }
  {
    thread_local S object_2("s", "t");
  }
  thread_local S object_3(".", "a");
  thread_local S object_4("o", "t");
  static S object_5("p", "s");
  thread_local S object_6(".", "s");
}

// Answer (12):

// __ __ __ __ __ __ __ __ __ __ __ __
```

Puzzle 81

```
void run() {
  static S object_1("c", "o");
  {
    thread_local S object_2("o", "l");
    static S object_3("n", "t");
    {
      thread_local S object_4("v", "b");
    }
    static S object_5("e", "_");
    thread_local S object_6("r", "i");
    static S object_7("t", "e");
  }
}

// Answer (14):

// __ __ __ __ __ __ __ __ __ __ __ __ __ __
```

Puzzle 82

```
void run() {
  static S object_1("d", "s");
  {
    static S object_2("e", "n");
  }
  {
    thread_local S object_3("p", "e");
    {
      static S object_4("r", "o");
      thread_local S object_5(".", "v");
    }
    static S object_6("c", "i");
  }
  static S object_7("o", "s");
  static S object_8("n", "r");
}

// Answer (16):

// __ __ __ __ __ __ __ __ __ __ __ __ __ __ __ __
```

Puzzle 83

```
void run() {
  thread_local S object_1("s", "e");
  static S object_2("p", "s");
  thread_local S object_3("a", "m");
  {
    static S object_4("n", "r");
    {
      thread_local S object_5("s", ".");
    }
    static S object_6("t", "e");
    thread_local S object_7("r", "m");
    static S object_8("e", "b");
  }
  {
    static S object_9("a", "m");
  }
}

// Answer (18):

// __ __ __ __ __ __ __ __ __ __ __ __ __ __ __ __ __ __
```

Puzzle 84

```
void run() {
  static S object_1("r", "r");
  {
    static S object_2("a", "o");
    thread_local S object_3("n", "a");
    {
      thread_local S object_4("g", "r");
    }
    {
      thread_local S object_5("e", "e");
      {
        thread_local S object_6(".", "t");
      }
      thread_local S object_7("s", "i");
      static S object_8("p", "t");
      thread_local S object_9("l", ".");
    }
```

```
    thread_local S object_10("i", "t");
  }
}

// Answer (20):

// __ __ __ __ __ __ __ __ __ __ __ __ __ __ __ __ __ __ __ __
```

Puzzle 85

```
void run() {
  S object_1("f", "n");
  S object_2("e", "u"); {
    S object_3("s", "e");
  }
thread_local S object_4("t", "d");
  S object_5("r", "o");
}

// Answer (10):

// __ __ __ __ __ __ __ __ __ __
```

Puzzle 86

```
void run() {
  {
    thread_local S object_1("c", "d");
  }
  thread_local S object_2("l", "n");
  {
    thread_local S object_3("a", "e");
    S object_4("s", "s");
  }
  thread_local S object_5(".", "i");
  S object_6("f", "r");
}

// Answer (12):

// __ __ __ __ __ __ __ __ __ __ __ __
```

Puzzle 87

```
void run() {
  {
    {
        thread_local S object_1("s", "o"); }
      thread_local S object_2("t", "i");
    thread_local S object_3("r", "."); S object_4("i", "n");
  }
  thread_local S object_5("g", "w");
  S object_6(".", "e");
  S object_7("v", "i");
}

// Answer (14):

// __ __ __ __ __ __ __ __ __ __ __ __ __ __
```

Puzzle 88

```
void run() {
  {
    thread_local S object_1("i", "s");
    {
      S object_2("f", "e");
      { thread_local S object_3("s", "r");
      } S object_4("t", "m");
      S object_5("r", ".");
      thread_local S object_6("e", "e");
      S object_7("a", "m");
    }
    S object_8("m", "b");
  }
}

// Answer (16):

// __ __ __ __ __ __ __ __ __ __ __ __ __ __ __ __
```

Puzzle 89

```
void run() {
  thread_local S object_1("c", "t"); thread_local S object_2("o", "s");
  {
    S object_3("u", "n"); }
  thread_local S object_4("t", "n");
  {
    S object_5("e", "e");
    { S object_6("d", "."); }
    S object_7("i", "t");
  }
thread_local S object_8("r", "o");
  thread_local S object_9(".", "c");
}

// Answer (18):

// __ __ __ __ __ __ __ __ __ __ __ __ __ __ __ __ __ __
```

Puzzle 90

```
void run() {
  thread_local S object_1("s", "e");
  {
    S object_2("h", "u");
  }
  thread_local S object_3("f", "n");
  S object_4("f", "n");
  {
    S object_5("l", "e");
    { S object_6("e", "d");
      thread_local S object_7("_", "i");
      S object_8("o", "r");
    }
    thread_local S object_9("e", "g");
    S object_10("r", "_");
  }
}

// Answer (20):

// __ __ __ __ __ __ __ __ __ __ __ __ __ __ __ __ __ __ __ __
```

Puzzle 91

```
void run() {
  S *object_1 = nullptr;
  {
    S *object_2 = new S("m", "a");
  }
  object_1 = new S("e", "m");
  delete object_1;
  S *object_3 = new S("_", "f");
  delete object_3;
  S *object_4 = nullptr;
  thread_local S object_5("u", "n");
}

// Answer (7):

// __ __ __ __ __ __ __
```

Puzzle 92

```
void run() {
  S *object_1 = nullptr;
  {
    S *object_2 = nullptr;
  }
  object_1 = new S("s", "t");
  {
    delete object_1;
  }
  thread_local S object_3("r", "m");
  S *object_4 = new S("s", "t");
  S *object_5 = nullptr;
  delete object_4;
  object_5 = new S("r", "e");
  delete object_5;
  S *object_6 = new S("a", "l");
}

// Answer (9):

// __ __ __ __ __ __ __ __ __
```

Puzzle 93

```
void run() {
  {
    S *object_1 = nullptr;
    object_1 = new S("b", "i");
  }
  S *object_2 = new S("a", "t");
  {
    thread_local S object_3("d", "d");
  }
  S *object_4 = nullptr;
  thread_local S object_5(".", "i");
  delete object_2;
  S *object_6 = new S("y", "e");
  object_4 = new S("p", "j");
  S *object_7 = new S("e", "h");
}

// Answer (10):

// __ __ __ __ __ __ __ __ __ __
```

Puzzle 94

```
void run() {
  {
    thread_local S object_1("r", "g");
    {
      thread_local S object_2("e", "a");
    }
  }
  S *object_3 = nullptr;
  S *object_4 = new S(".", "m");
  delete object_4;
  S *object_5 = nullptr;
  object_3 = new S("a", "s");
  thread_local S object_6("t", "l");
  S *object_7 = new S("c", "t");
  thread_local S object_8("h", "f");
}

// Answer (12):
```

```
// __ __ __ __ __ __ __ __ __ __ __ __
```

Puzzle 95

```
void run() {
  {
    S *object_1 = nullptr;
    object_1 = new S("c", "a");
    S *object_2 = nullptr;
  }
  S *object_3 = new S("o", "u");
  S *object_4 = nullptr;
  delete object_3;
  object_4 = new S("n", "i");
  {
    thread_local S object_5("t", "e");
    {
      S *object_6 = new S("l", "d");
      S *object_7 = nullptr;
      S *object_8 = new S("_", "s");
      thread_local S object_9("o", "n");
    }
  }
}

// Answer (10):

// __ __ __ __ __ __ __ __ __ __
```

Puzzle 96

```
void run() {
  S *object_1 = nullptr;
  object_1 = new S("f", "s");
  delete object_1;
  S *object_2 = new S(".", "n");
  S *object_3 = nullptr;
  thread_local S object_4("e", "t");
  {
    object_3 = new S("r", ".");
    S *object_5 = new S("r", "p");
  }
```

```
  delete object_3;
  {
    S *object_6 = nullptr;
    S *object_7 = new S("r", "q");
    object_6 = new S("e", "p");
    {
      {
      }
      S *object_8 = nullptr;
      delete object_6;
      thread_local S object_9("o", "r");
    }
    S *object_10 = nullptr;
  }
}

// Answer (13):

// __ __ __ __ __ __ __ __ __ __ __ __ __
```

Puzzle 97

```
void run() {
  thread_local S object_1("u", "t");
  S *object_2 = nullptr;
  thread_local S object_3("i", "_");
  S object_4("n", "2");
  object_2 = new S("t", "o");
  S *object_5 = new S("3", "g");
}

// Answer (8):

// __ __ __ __ __ __ __ __
```

Puzzle 98

```
void run() {
  {
    S *object_1 = nullptr;
    thread_local S object_2("w", "b");
    object_1 = new S("c", "x");
    S *object_3 = nullptr;
    thread_local S object_4("t", "m");
    S *object_5 = nullptr;
    S *object_6 = new S("o", "j");
  }
}

// Answer (6):

// __ __ __ __ __ __
```

Puzzle 99

```
void run() {
  S *object_1 = nullptr;
  S object_2("t", "i");
  thread_local S object_3("e", "s");
  object_1 = new S("m", "a");
  S object_4("p", "l");
  {
    thread_local S object_5(".", "a");
  }
  S *object_6 = new S("a", "p");
  S *object_7 = nullptr;
}

// Answer (10):

// __ __ __ __ __ __ __ __ __ __
```

Puzzle 100

```
void run() {
  {
    {
      thread_local S object_1("s", "f");
      {
        S *object_2 = nullptr;
        S *object_3 = new S("t", "s");
        object_2 = new S("r", "d");
        delete object_3;
      }
      S *object_4 = nullptr;
      thread_local S object_5("t", "u");
      S object_6("r", "m");
      thread_local S object_7("e", "b");
      S *object_8 = new S("a", "i");
    }
  }
}

// Answer (12):

// __ __ __ __ __ __ __ __ __ __ __ __
```

Puzzle 101

```
void run() {
  thread_local S object_1("c", "d");
  {
    S *object_2 = new S("f", "b");
    {
      thread_local S object_3("e", "a");
      {
        S *object_4 = nullptr;
        S *object_5 = new S("n", "u");
      }
      S *object_6 = new S("v", "v");
    }
    S object_7(".", "e");
    S *object_8 = new S("t", "q");
    S object_9("h", "r");
  }
```

```
}

// Answer (12):

// __ __ __ __ __ __ __ __ __ __ __ __
```

Puzzle 102

```
void run() {
  {
    thread_local S object_1("c", "d");
    S *object_2 = nullptr;
  }
  S *object_3 = new S("o", "c");
  S *object_4 = nullptr;
  S *object_5 = new S("p", "h");
  {
    S object_6("y", "_");
  }
  S *object_7 = new S("b", "d");
  S object_8("a", "r");
  {
    delete object_3;
    S object_9("k", "a");
    S *object_10 = new S("w", "p");
  }
}

// Answer (13):

// __ __ __ __ __ __ __ __ __ __ __ __ __
```

Puzzle 103

```
void run() {
  {
  }
  S *object_1 = nullptr;
  object_1 = new S("b", "i");
  delete object_1;
  thread_local S object_2("n", "d");
  S *object_3 = new S("d", "r");
  /* ________ */
```

```
  /* ________ */
  S *object_5 = new S("2", "y");
}

// Answer (9):

// binder2nd
```

Puzzle 104

```
void run() {
  {
    {
      S *object_1 = nullptr;
      /* ________ */
      S *object_3 = nullptr;
      object_1 = new S("t", "t");
      S *object_4 = nullptr;
      /* ________ */
      thread_local S object_6("t", "l");
    }
  }
}

// Answer (7):

// strtold
```

Puzzle 105

```
void run() {
  {
    S object_1("i", "i");
    /* ________ */
    {
      S *object_3 = nullptr;
    }
    /* ________ */
    thread_local S object_4("n", "y");
    S *object_5 = nullptr;
    thread_local S object_6("t", "t");
    S *object_7 = nullptr;
  }
```

```
}

// Answer (8):

// identity
```

Puzzle 106

```
void run() {
  /* ________ */
  thread_local S object_2("e", "c");
  /* ________ */
  /* ________ */
  {
    S *object_5 = new S("r", "p");
  }
  {
    S *object_6 = new S("e", "k");
  }
  S object_7("s", "u");
  delete object_3;
  {
    thread_local S object_8("p", "i");
  }
}

// Answer (14):

// mem.res.public
```

Puzzle 107

```
void run() {
  /* ________ */
  S *object_2 = nullptr;
  /* ________ */
  S *object_4 = nullptr;
  S *object_5 = new S("g", "x");
  {
    S object_6(".", "r");
    {
      thread_local S object_7("s", "h");
      {
```

```
        S *object_8 = nullptr;
        object_2 = new S("e", "n");
      }
      /* ________ */
    }
  }
}

// Answer (10):

// alg.search
```

Puzzle 108

```
void run() {
  /* ________ */
  S *object_2 = nullptr;
  S object_3("t", "e");
  {
  }
  /* ________ */
  {
    S *object_4 = nullptr;
    {
      delete object_2;
    }
    object_4 = new S("k", "q");
    /* ________ */
    S object_6("r", ".");
    {
      thread_local S object_7("a", "r");
    }
    S object_8("c", "e");
  }
  S *object_9 = nullptr;
  object_9 = new S("g", "f");
  S object_10("e", "n");
}

// Answer (18):

// stacktrace.general
```

Puzzle 109

```
void run() {
  S *object_1 = new S("c", "s");
  S *object_2 = nullptr;
  S *object_3 = new S("o", "w");
  S *object_4 = nullptr;
  object_4 = new S("d", "y");
  {
    S *object_5 = new S("e", "g"); thread_local S object_6("c", "e");
  }
  S *object_7 = new S("v", "h");
  {
    S("t", "_");
    S *object_9 = new S("b", "u");
    S object_10("a", "s");
  }
}

// Answer (12):

// __ __ __ __ __ __ __ __ __ __ __ __
```

Puzzle 110

```
void run() {
  S object_1("f", ".");
  S *object_2 = new S("s", "y");
  S object_3(".", "m");
  S *object_4 = new S("f", "e");
  S *object_5 = nullptr;
  S object_6("i", "e");
  S *object_7 = nullptr;
  static S object_8("l", "n");
  {
    delete object_4;
  }
  static S object_9("s", "y");
  delete object_2;
  S *object_10 = new S("s", "f");
  thread_local S object_11("t", "s");
}
```

```
// Answer (17):

// __ __ __ __ __ __ __ __ __ __ __ __ __ __ __ __ __
```

Puzzle 111

```
void run() {
  static S object_1("t", "e");
  thread_local S object_2("h", "d");
  thread_local S object_3("r", "n");
  new S("e", "x");
  thread_local S object_5("a", "a");
  S *object_6 = nullptr;
  thread_local S object_7("d", "h"); S *object_8 = new S(":", "i");
  {
    S object_9(":", "e");
    static S object_10("n", "l");
    object_6 = new S("a", "b");
    thread_local S object_11("t", "_");
    S("i", "v");
  }
}

// Answer (21):

// __ __ __ __ __ __ __ __ __ __ __ __ __ __ __ __ __ __ __ __ __
```

Puzzle 112

```
void run() {
  static S object_1("d", "e");
  S object_2("e", "i");
  thread_local S object_3("f", "t");
  {
    thread_local S object_4("n", ".");
    S *object_5 = new S("s", "y");
    new S(".", "u");
    thread_local S object_7("d", "c");
    {
      delete object_5;
    }
    S *object_8 = nullptr;
    {
```

```
      S *object_9 = nullptr;
      {
        static S object_10("n", "p");
        S *object_11 = nullptr;
        static S object_12("a", "y");
        S *object_13 = new S("m", "r");
      }
    }
  }
}

// Answer (18):

// __ __ __ __ __ __ __ __ __ __ __ __ __ __ __ __ __ __
```

Puzzle 113

```
void run() {
  static S object_1("d", "d");
  S *object_2 = nullptr;
  S *object_3 = new S("e", "i");
  static S object_4("r", "i");
  delete object_3;
  delete new S("v", "e");
  {
    new S("d", "y");
    S object_7(" ", "f");
    object_2 = new S("t", "y");
    delete object_2;
    S *object_8 = nullptr;
    S *object_9 = new S("p", "e");
    delete object_9;
    static S object_10(" ", "e");
  }
  S object_11("o", "p");
  S *object_12 = nullptr;
  S("r", " ");
  S object_14("t", "y");
}

// Answer (23):

// __ __ __ __ __ __ __ __ __ __ __ __ __ __ __ __ __ __ __ __ __ __ __
```

Puzzle 114

```
void run() {
  new S("t", "f");
  {
    S object_2("i", "l");
    {
      S *object_3 = new S("m", "p");
      S object_4("e", ".");
    }
    thread_local S object_5("c", "r");
    static S object_6("a", "s");
  }
  S *object_7 = nullptr;
  thread_local S object_8(".", "e");
  object_7 = new S("m", "o");
  delete object_7;
  S object_9("n", "b");
  {
    S *object_10 = new S("t", "q");
    S object_11("h", ".");
  }
  S *object_12 = nullptr;
  object_12 = new S("m", "x");
  S("e", "m");
  S *object_14 = nullptr;
  {
    S *object_15 = nullptr;
  }
}

// Answer (22):

// __ __ __ __ __ __ __ __ __ __ __ __ __ __ __ __ __ __ __ __ __ __
```

Puzzle 115

```
void run() {
  S *object_1 = new S("s", "r");
  thread_local S object_2("y", "m"); static S object_3("s", "s");
    thread_local S object_4("e", "e");
  {
    thread_local S object_5("r", "m");
    S *object_6 = nullptr;
    thread_local S object_7("r", "n");
    S *object_8 = new S(".", "v");
    thread_local S object_9("e", "o");
  }
  S *object_10 = nullptr;
  delete object_1;
  S *object_11 = new S("r", "h");
  static S object_12("c", "r");
  S *object_13 = new S("o", "d");
  static S object_14("n", "e");
  delete object_13;
  {
    S object_15("i", "t");
  }
  S object_16("i", "n");
  {
    S object_17("o", ".");
    static S object_18("n", "b");
  }
}

// Answer (30):

// __ __ __ __ __ __ __ __ __ __ __ __ __ __ __ __ __ __ __ __ __ __ __ __
//
// __ __ __ __ __ __
```

Puzzle 116

```
void run() {
  thread_local S object_1("t", "v");
  {
    static S object_2("e", "w");
    S *object_3 = new S("m", "r");
    S *object_4 = nullptr;
    S object_5("p", "a");
    S *object_6 = nullptr;
    object_6 = new S("l", "v");
  }
  S object_7("t", "o"); static S object_8("e", "e");
  {
    thread_local S object_9(".", "r");
    thread_local S object_10("g", "e");
  }
  S *object_11 = new S("s", "i");
  thread_local S object_12("l", "v");
  {
    S("i", "c");
  }
  S object_14("e", ".");
    S *object_15 = new S(".", "m");
  {
    S *object_16 = new S("a", "t");
    {
      S *object_17 = nullptr;
    }
    static S object_18("r", "i");
    {
      S object_19("r", "y");
      S *object_20 = new S("a", "h");
    }
  }
}

// Answer (30):

// __ __ __ __ __ __ __ __ __ __ __ __ __ __ __ __ __ __ __ __ __ __ __ __
//
// __ __ __ __ __ __
```

Puzzle 117

```
void run() {
  S *object_1 = new S("i", "i");
  S *object_2 = nullptr;
  {
    thread_local S object_3("s", "l");
  }
  S object_4("_", "t");
  S *object_5 = nullptr;
  S *object_6 = new S("t", "j");
  S object_7("r", "c");
  S *object_8 = nullptr;
  object_8 = new S("i", "w");
  static S object_9("v", "v");
  S *object_10 = nullptr;
  S *object_11 = nullptr;
  new S("i", "v");
  static S object_13("a", "_");
  object_2 = new S("l", "f");
  {
    S object_14("l", "e");
    object_5 = new S("y", "v");
  S object_15("_", "d");
  }
  S("f", "a");
  thread_local S object_17("u", "b");
  S object_18("l", "u");
  object_11 = new S("t", "a");
  {
    static S object_19("_", "e");
    object_10 = new S("c", "t");
    S object_20("o", "r");
    S *object_21 = new S("n", "t");
    thread_local S object_22("s", "i");
    S *object_23 = new S("t", "k");
  }
}

// Answer (36):

// __ __ __ __ __ __ __ __ __ __ __ __ __ __ __ __ __ __ __ __ __ __ __ __
//
```

```
// __ __ __ __ __ __ __ __ __ __ __ __
```

Puzzle 118

```
void run() {
  S object_1("t", "_");
  { thread_local S object_2("y", "r");
    S *object_3 = nullptr;
    S *object_4 = new S("p", "r");
    static S object_5("e", "r");
    S object_6(" ", "o");
  }
  {
    static S object_7("f", "o");
    delete new S(" ", "u");
    S object_9("n", "d");
    {
      static S object_10("o", "t");
    }
    S *object_11 = nullptr;
    S *object_12 = new S("r", "b");
  }
  thread_local S object_13("e", "e");
  S("r", "e");
  {
    S object_15("d", "_");
  }
{
    delete new S("m", "u");
    S *object_17 = new S("l", "t");
    S *object_18 = nullptr;
    {
      delete object_17;
    }
    {
      new S("i", "v");
      thread_local S object_20("s", "t");
    }
    S("e", "t");
    S object_22(":", "l");
    thread_local S object_23(":", "i");
    {
      object_18 = new S("l", "a");
```

```
      static S object_24("o", "a");
      S("c", "a");
    }
  }
}

// Answer (42):

// __ __ __ __ __ __ __ __ __ __ __ __ __ __ __ __ __ __ __ __ __ __ __ __
//
// __ __ __ __ __ __ __ __ __ __ __ __ __ __ __ __ __ __
```

Puzzle 119

```
void run() {
    S *object_1 = new S("v", "l");
  thread_local S object_2("a", "a");
  S *object_3 = nullptr;
  {
    S *object_4 = nullptr;
    delete object_1;
    {
      object_4 = new S("u", "t");
      static S object_5("e", "s");
      S *object_6 = new S("s", "_");
      {
        S object_7(" ", " ");
        S *object_8 = new S("o", "r");
        object_3 = new S("f", "A");
      }
      S *object_9 = new S("v", "O");
      S *object_10 = nullptr;
      {
        thread_local S object_11("a", "m");
        {
          static S object_12("r", "o");
          delete new S("i", "o");
          S object_14("u", "T");
          object_10 = new S("s", "C");
          new S(" ", "j");
          delete object_3;
        }
        S object_16("O", ".");
```

```
        new S("M", "f");
        thread_local S object_18("I", " ");
        S *object_19 = new S("C", ".");
        S *object_20 = nullptr;
        delete object_6;
        {
          static S object_21(".", "r");
        }
        S *object_22 = nullptr;
        delete object_19;
      }
      S("_", "L");
      {
        delete object_9;
        delete object_10;
        S *object_24 = nullptr;
      } S *object_25 = new S("K", "y");
    }
    S object_26("_", "E");
    static S object_27("F", "c");
    thread_local S object_28("R", "E");
  }
}

// Answer (45):

// __ __ __ __ __ __ __ __ __ __ __ __ __ __ __ __ __ __ __ __ __ __ __ __
//
// __ __ __ __ __ __ __ __ __ __ __ __ __ __ __ __ __ __ __ __ __
```

Puzzle 120

```
void run() {
  thread_local S object_1("A", "b"); S *object_2 = new S(" ", "b");
  thread_local S object_3("c", "a");
  delete new S("a", "l");
  {
    static S object_5("l", ".");
  }
  delete new S("a", "b");
  S("l", "e");
  S *object_8 = nullptr;
  static S object_9(" ", "e");
```

```
  S *object_10 = new S("o", " ");
  delete object_2;
  thread_local S object_11("j", "l");
  static S object_12("e", "p");
  S *object_13 = nullptr;
  thread_local S object_14("c", "l");
  static S object_15("t", "y");
  object_13 = new S(" ", "i"); delete object_13;
  S *object_16 = new S("s", "v");
  delete object_10;
  S("a", "n");
  S *object_18 = nullptr;
  S *object_19 = new S(" ", "o");
  object_18 = new S("o", "t");
  S *object_20 = new S("b", "w");
  S *object_21 = nullptr;
static S object_22("j", "t");
  static S object_23("e", " "); S object_24("c", "a");
  S object_25("t", "c");
  static S object_26(" ", "e");
  S object_27("o", " ");
S *object_28 = new S("f", "d");
  new S(" ", "n");
  static S object_30("a", "l");
}

// Answer (50):

// __ __ __ __ __ __ __ __ __ __ __ __ __ __ __ __ __ __ __ __ __ __ __ __
//
// __ __ __ __ __ __ __ __ __ __ __ __ __ __ __ __ __ __ __ __ __ __ __ __
//
// __ __
```

Puzzle 121

```
void run() {
  S object_1("s", "e");
  S *object_2 = new S("y", "a");
  {
    S *object_3 = nullptr;
  }
  static S object_4("n", "w");
  S object_5("c", "v");
  S *object_6 = new S("s", "y");
  {
    S object_7("t", "o");
    delete new S("r", "e");
    S("a", "m");
    S *object_10 = nullptr;
    /* ________ */
    thread_local S object_12("o", "v");
    delete new S("s", "y");
    {
      object_10 = new S("n", "i");
      {
        /* ________ */
      }
      new S("t", "d");
      static S object_16("r", "i");
    }
    {
      /* ________ */
    }
    delete object_2;
    S object_18("m", ".");
  }
}

// Answer (31):

// syncstream.osyncstream.overview
```

Puzzle 122

```
void run() {
  S *object_1 = nullptr;
  /* ________ */
  {
    S object_3("o", "_");
    {
      S *object_4 = new S("u", "c");
      /* ________ */
      {
        /* ________ */
        S *object_6 = new S("e", "n");
        {
          S("_", "l");
        }
        {
          S *object_8 = new S("o", "i");
        }
        S object_9("c", "o");
        thread_local S object_10("a", "n");
        delete new S("t", "i");
        {
          S *object_12 = new S("o", "p");
          {
            static S object_13("n", "e");
            S *object_14 = nullptr;
            S(":", ":");
            delete new S("f", "u");
            /* ________ */
            S *object_17 = new S("c", "d");
            static S object_18("t", "m");
            S *object_19 = new S("i", "n");
          }
          {
            S *object_20 = nullptr;
          }
        }
      }
    }
  }
}
```

```
// Answer (30):

// source_location::function_name
```

Puzzle 123

```
void run() {
  S("t", "y");
  S *object_2 = nullptr;
  thread_local S object_3("p", "t");
  S *object_4 = new S("e", "o");
  object_2 = new S(" ", "n");
  delete object_4;
  S *object_5 = nullptr;
  static S object_6("f", "e");
  S *object_7 = new S(" ", "m");
  /* ________ */
  delete object_2;
  thread_local S object_9("o", "e");
  S *object_10 = nullptr;
  object_5 = new S("r", "e");
  thread_local S object_11("d", "c");
  /* ________ */
  delete object_5;
  S *object_13 = nullptr;
  /* ________ */
  delete object_7;
  new S("a", "y");
  object_13 = new S("p", ":");
  delete object_13;
  S *object_16 = new S(":", "e");
  thread_local S object_17("d", "n");
  {
    object_10 = new S("i", "f");
  }
  {
    {
      S *object_18 = nullptr;
      delete object_10;
    }
    static S object_19("f", "p");
    {
      static S object_20("e", "y");
```

```
    }
    /* ________ */
  }
}

// Answer (38):

// type of unordered_map::difference_type
```

Puzzle 124

```
void run() {
  /* ________ */
  static S object_2("n", "r");
  S *object_3 = nullptr;
  S *object_4 = new S("i", "f");
  static S object_5("t", "c");
  S object_6(" ", " ");
  S("s", "u");
  S *object_8 = nullptr;
  delete object_4;
  {
    object_3 = new S("f", "t");
    S object_9("i", "o");
    static S object_10("x", "i");
    thread_local S object_11(" ", "s");
    /* ________ */
    /* ________ */
    {
      object_8 = new S("e", "s");
    }
    /* ________ */
    S *object_15 = new S(" ", "k");
    S object_16("P", "i");
    S *object_17 = nullptr;
    {
      S *object_18 = nullptr;
    }
    S("e", "r");
  }
  S object_20("d", "e");
  static S object_21(":", " ");
  S object_22(":", "p");
```

```
  /* ________ */
}

// Answer (38):

// unit suffix when Period::type is micro
```

Puzzle 125

```
void run() {
  /* ________ */
  S object_2("l", "o");
  {
    S("i", "g");
  }
  S *object_4 = nullptr;
  delete object_1;
  static S object_5("m", "t");
  S object_6("e", " ");
  /* ________ */
  S object_7("t", "s");
  static S object_8(" ", "c");
  S object_9("o", "s");
  delete object_4;
  {
    S *object_10 = new S(" ", "f");
    S object_11("b", "t");
    static S object_12("i", "e");
  }
  /* ________ */
  new S("i", "i");
  S *object_15 = new S("e", " ");
  {
    S("l", "d");
    S *object_17 = new S("s", "w");
  }
  delete object_15;
  S("w", "i");
  S *object_19 = new S("t", "i");
  thread_local S object_20("h", "b");
  delete object_19;
  new S("n", "r");
  /* ________ */
```

```
  {
  }
  /* ________ */
  {
    S *object_24 = new S(" ", "a");
  }
  S object_25("c", "l");
}

// Answer (45):

// alignment of bit-fields within a class object
```

Puzzle 126

```
void run() {
  /* ________ */
  {
    {
      S *object_2 = new S("f", "x");
      /* ________ */
      thread_local S object_4("l", "l");
      static S object_5("t", "t");
    }
    {
      S *object_6 = new S(" ", "i");
    }
    /* ________ */
  }
  static S object_8("m", "e");
  {
  }
  new S("b", "k");
  /* ________ */
  S *object_11 = new S("r", "f");
  S object_12(" ", "m");
  new S("o", "x");
  delete object_11;
  static S object_14(" ", "i");
  S object_15("b", "_");
  {
    S object_16("u", "c");
  }
```

```
  S("k", "e");
  S *object_18 = new S("t", "s");
  delete object_18;
  S *object_19 = nullptr;
  {
    static S object_20(" ", "t");
    S object_21("i", "r");
    /* ________ */
    {
      object_19 = new S(" ", "o");
      delete new S("u", "n");
      delete object_19;
    }
    S *object_24 = nullptr;
  }
  S("d", "e");
  /* ________ */
  S object_27("e", "d");
}

// Answer (47):

// default number of buckets in unordered_multiset
```

Puzzle 127

```
void run() {
  thread_local S object_1("r", "w");
  {
    S *object_2 = new S("e", "a");
  }
  S object_3("t", "c");
  new S("u", "t");
  {
    S *object_5 = new S("r", " ");
    /* ________ */
    {
      delete object_5;
      S *object_7 = nullptr;
      {
        thread_local S object_8("v", ":");
        /* ________ */
        S *object_10 = nullptr;
```

```
      /* ________ */
      S object_12("u", "e");
    }
    thread_local S object_13("o", ":");
    S *object_14 = new S("f", " ");
    delete object_14;
    /* ________ */
    S object_16("a", "o");
    S *object_17 = nullptr;
    thread_local S object_18("d", "s");
    object_7 = new S("_", "n");
  }
  {
    static S object_19("p", "a");
    thread_local S object_20("t", "e");
    S *object_21 = nullptr;
  }
  S *object_22 = new S("i", "o");
  /* ________ */
}
S *object_23 = nullptr;
static S object_24("n", "h");
S object_25("a", "c");
/* ________ */
S *object_27 = new S("a", "g");
S *object_28 = nullptr;
}

// Answer (41):

// return value of bad_optional_access::what
```

Puzzle 128

```
void run() {
  /* ________ */
  thread_local S object_2("f", " ");
  /* ________ */
  S object_4("c", "t");
  static S object_5("t", "8");
  S *object_6 = nullptr;
  S *object_7 = new S(" ", "c");
  /* ________ */
```

```
S *object_8 = nullptr;
S object_9("f", "i");
{
  static S object_10(" ", "2");
}
/* ________ */
thread_local S object_11("a", "n");
{
  S object_12("l", "w");
  {
    S *object_13 = nullptr;
    /* ________ */
    {
      object_8 = new S("i", "e");
      thread_local S object_15("n", " ");
    }
    /* ________ */
    {
      /* ________ */
      S object_18("L", "u");
      static S object_19("a", "=");
      delete object_6;
    }
    delete object_8;
    S object_20("r", "y");
    object_13 = new S("r", "k");
    S object_21("e", "l");
    S(" ", "p");
    thread_local S object_23("o", "h");
  }
  {
    S object_24("o", " ");
    {
      S *object_25 = nullptr;
      {
        delete new S("m", "i");
        static S object_27("a", ">");
        S *object_28 = nullptr;
      }
      new S("l", "o");
    }
    S *object_30 = new S("s", "o");
  }
```

```
  }
}

// Answer (52):

// effect of calling Laguerre polynomials with n >= 128
```

Solutions

Solution 1

```
void run() {
  S object_1("a", "n");                          // a
  S object_2("s", "i");                          // s
}                                                // i
                                                 // n

// Answer: asin
```

Solution 2

```
void run() {
  {
    S object_1("e", "t");                        // e
    {
      S object_2("x", "t");                      // x
    }                                            // t
    S object_3("e", "n");                        // e
  }                                              // n
                                                 // t
}

// Answer: extent
```

Solution 3

```
void run() {
  S object_1("p", "t");                          // p
  {
    S object_2("o", "n");                        // o
    {
      S object_3("p", "c");                      // p
    }                                            // c
    S object_4("o", "u");                        // o
  }                                              // u
                                                 // n
}                                                // t
```

```
// Answer: popcount
```

Solution 4

```
void run() {
  {
    {
      S object_1("t", "c");                    // t
      {
        S object_2("e", "m");                  // e
      }                                        // m
      S object_3("p", ".");                    // p
    }                                          // .
                                               // c
    S object_4("l", "a");                      // l
  }                                            // a
  S object_5("s", "s");                        // s
}                                              // s

// Answer: temp.class
```

Solution 5

```
void run() {
  {
    S object_1("r", "a");                      // r
  }                                            // a
  {
    S object_2("n", "g");                      // n
  }                                            // g
  S object_3("e", "f");                        // e
  {
    S object_4("s", ":");                      // s
  }                                            // :
  S object_5(":", "o");                        // :
  S object_6("a", "_");                        // a
  S object_7("n", "y");                        // n
}                                              // y
                                               // _
                                               // o
                                               // f
```

```
// Answer: ranges::any_of
```

Solution 6

```
void run() {
  {
    {
      S object_1("c", "c");                          // c
      {
        S object_2("o", "t");                        // o
        {
          S object_3("n", "c");                      // n
        }                                            // c
        S object_4("e", "p");                        // e
      }                                              // p
                                                     // t
      S object_5("s", ".");                          // s
    }                                                // .
                                                     // c
    S object_6("o", "m");                            // o
  }                                                  // m
  S object_7("p", "e");                              // p
  S object_8("a", "r");                              // a
}                                                    // r
                                                     // e

// Answer: concepts.compare
```

Solution 7

```
void run() {
  {
    S object_1("c", "u");                            // c
    {
      S object_2("o", "p");                          // o
    }                                                // p
    {
      S object_3("y", "s");                          // y
      {
        S object_4("_", "c");                        // _
      }                                              // c
      S object_5("o", "n");                          // o
```

```
    }                                               // n
                                                    // s
    S object_6("t", "r");                           // t
  }                                                 // r
                                                    // u
  S object_7("c", "e");                             // c
  S object_8("t", "l");                             // t
  S object_9("i", "b");                             // i
}                                                   // b
                                                    // l
                                                    // e

// Answer: copy_constructible
```

Solution 8

```
void run() {
  {
    S object_1("t", "h");                           // t
  }                                                 // h
  {
    S object_2("r", ".");                           // r
    {
      S object_3("e", "a");                         // e
    }                                               // a
    {
      S object_4("d", "e");                         // d
      {
        S object_5(".", "t");                       // .
      }                                             // t
      S object_6("h", "r");                         // h
    }                                               // r
                                                    // e
    S object_7("a", "d");                           // a
  }                                                 // d
                                                    // .
  S object_8("s", "c");                             // s
  S object_9("t", "i");                             // t
  S object_10("a", "t");                            // a
}                                                   // t
                                                    // i
                                                    // c
```

```
// Answer: thread.thread.static
```

Solution 9

```
void run() {
  {
    S object_1("m", "o");                       // m
  }                                             // o
  S object_2("v", "e");                         // v
}                                               // e

// Answer: move
```

Solution 10

```
void run() {
  {
    {
      S object_1("g", "r");                     // g
    }                                           // r
    S object_2("a", "m");                       // a
  }                                             // m
  S object_3(".", "s");                         // .
  S object_4("c", "s");                         // c
  S object_5("l", "a");                         // l
}                                               // a
                                                // s
                                                // s

// Answer: gram.class
```

Solution 11

```
void run() {
  {
    S object_1("h", "a");                       // h
  }                                             // a
  {
    S object_2("s", "b");                       // s
    {
      S object_3("_", "l");                     // _
```

```
      {
        S object_4("s", "i");                        // s
      }                                              // i
      S object_5("n", "g");                          // n
    }                                                // g
                                                     // l
    S object_6("e", "_");                            // e
  }                                                  // _
                                                     // b
  S object_7("i", "t");                              // i
}                                                    // t

// Answer: has_single_bit
```

Solution 12

```
void run() {
  {
    {
      S object_1("r", "g");                          // r
      {
        S object_2("a", "n");                        // a
      }                                              // n
      S object_3("g", ".");                          // g
      {
        S object_4("e", "e");                        // e
        {
          S object_5(".", "a");                      // .
        }                                            // a
        S object_6("c", "c");                        // c
      }                                              // c
                                                     // e
      S object_7("s", "s");                          // s
    }                                                // s
                                                     // .
                                                     // g
    S object_8("e", "n");                            // e
  }                                                  // n
  S object_9("e", "l");                              // e
  S object_10("r", "a");                             // r
}                                                    // a
                                                     // l
```

```
// Answer: range.access.general
```

Solution 13

```
void run() {
  static S object_1("w", "f");                    // w
  {
    static S object_2("c", "o");                  // c
  }
  static S object_3("s", "t");                    // s
}

// Program Exit
// t
// o
// f

// Answer: wcstof
```

Solution 14

```
void run() {
  {
    static S object_1("o", "b");                  // o
    {
      static S object_2("v", "u");                // v
    }
    static S object_3("e", "s");                  // e
  }
  static S object_4("r", ".");                    // r
}

// Program Exit
// .
// s
// u
// b

// Answer: over.sub
```

Solution 15

```
void run() {
  {
    static S object_1("d", "t");                    // d
  }
  {
    static S object_2("y", "s");                    // y
  }
  static S object_3("n", "a");                      // n
  static S object_4("a", "c");                      // a
  static S object_5("m", "_");                      // m
  static S object_6("i", "c");                      // i
}

// Program Exit
// c
// _
// c
// a
// s
// t

// Answer: dynamic_cast
```

Solution 16

```
void run() {
  static S object_1("s", "d");                      // s
  static S object_2("e", "e");                      // e
  {
    static S object_3("t", "t");                    // t
    {
      static S object_4("_", "c");                  // _
    }
    {
      static S object_5("u", "e");                  // u
    }
    static S object_6("n", "p");                    // n
  }
  static S object_7("e", "x");                      // e
}
```

```
// Program Exit
// x
// p
// e
// c
// t
// e
// d

// Answer: set_unexpected
```

Solution 17

```
void run() {
  {
    static S object_1("f", "p");              // f
  }
  {
    static S object_2("u", "a");              // u
    {
      static S object_3("n", "c");            // n
    }
    static S object_4("c", ".");              // c
  }
  static S object_5(".", "c");                // .
  static S object_6("w", "n");                // w
  static S object_7("r", "u");                // r
  static S object_8("a", "f");                // a
  static S object_9("p", ".");                // p
}

// Program Exit
// .
// f
// u
// n
// c
// .
// c
// a
// p

// Answer: func.wrap.func.cap
```

Solution 18

```
void run() {
  {
    static S object_1("r", "w");                    // r
  }
  static S object_2("a", "e");                      // a
  {
    static S object_3("n", "i");                    // n
  }
  static S object_4("g", "v");                      // g
  {
    static S object_5("e", "r");                    // e
    {
      static S object_6(".", "e");                  // .
    }
    static S object_7("s", "v");                    // s
  }
  static S object_8("p", "o");                      // p
  static S object_9("l", ".");                      // l
  static S object_10("i", "t");                     // i
}

// Program Exit
// t
// .
// o
// v
// e
// r
// v
// i
// e
// w

// Answer: range.split.overview
```

Solution 19

```
void run() {
  {
    static S object_1("g", "f");                // g
  }
  S object_2("e", "_");                         // e
  static S object_3("t", "i");                  // t
}                                               // _

// Program Exit
// i
// f

// Answer: get_if
```

Solution 20

```
void run() {
  {
    {
      S object_1("m", "b");                     // m
    }                                           // b
    static S object_2("r", "6");                // r
  }
  S object_3("t", "1");                         // t
  S object_4("o", "c");                         // o
}                                               // c
                                                // 1

// Program Exit
// 6

// Answer: mbrtoc16
```

Solution 21

```
void run() {
  S object_1("m", "o");                         // m
  static S object_2("e", "r");                  // e
  {
    static S object_3("m", "e");                // m
  }
  {
    static S object_4("o", "d");                // o
    S object_5("r", "y");                       // r
  }                                             // y
  static S object_6("_", "r");                  // _
}                                               // o

// Program Exit
// r
// d
// e
// r

// Answer: memory_order
```

Solution 22

```
void run() {
  static S object_1("u", "p");                  // u
  S object_2("n", "i");                         // n
  {
    S object_3("o", "m");                       // o
    static S object_4("r", "a");                // r
    S object_5("d", ".");                       // d
  }                                             // .
                                                // m
  {
    static S object_6("u", "m");                // u
    S object_7("l", "t");                       // l
  }                                             // t
}                                               // i

// Program Exit
// m
// a
```

```
// p

// Answer: unord.multimap
```

Solution 23

```
void run() {
  {
    static S object_1("b", "t");              // b
  }
  S object_2("a", "p");                       // a
  {
    S object_3("s", "o");                     // s
    {
      S object_4("i", "_");                   // i
      static S object_5("c", "m");            // c
    }                                         // _
    static S object_6("i", "f");              // i
  }                                           // o
  S object_7("s", "o");                       // s
  static S object_8(":", "y");                // :
  S object_9(":", "c");                       // :
}                                             // c
                                              // o
                                              // p

// Program Exit
// y
// f
// m
// t

// Answer: basic_ios::copyfmt
```

Solution 24

```
void run() {
  {
    {
      S object_1("t", "i");                       // t
    }                                             // i
    static S object_2("m", "s");                  // m
  }
  static S object_3("e", "r");                    // e
  {
    static S object_4(".", "e");                  // .
    {
      static S object_5("c", "b");                // c
    }
    S object_6("a", "l");                         // a
  }                                               // l
  S object_7(".", "m");                           // .
  static S object_8("y", "m");                    // y
  S object_9("m", ".");                           // m
  static S object_10("d", "e");                   // d
}                                                 // .
                                                  // m

// Program Exit
// e
// m
// b
// e
// r
// s

// Answer: time.cal.ymd.members
```

Solution 25

```
void run() {
  {
    static S object_1("s", "h");                    // s
    S object_2("e", "a");                           // e
  }                                                 // a
  static S object_3("r", "c");                      // r
}

// Program Exit
// c
// h

// Answer: search
```

Solution 26

```
void run() {
  {
    static S object_1("d", "k");                    // d
  }
  static S object_2("e", "c");                      // e
  S object_3("f", "o");                             // f
  {
    S object_4("e", "r");                           // e
  }                                                 // r
  S object_5("_", "l");                             // _
}                                                   // l
                                                    // o

// Program Exit
// c
// k

// Answer: defer_lock
```

Solution 27

```
void run() {
  S object_1("d", "t");                         // d
  {
    static S object_2("e", "n");                // e
  }
  static S object_3("f", "o");                  // f
  {
    S object_4("n", "s");                       // n
  }                                             // s
  {
    S object_5(".", "p");                       // .
  }                                             // p
  S object_6("r", "c");                         // r
  static S object_7("o", "i");                  // o
  S object_8("j", "e");                         // j
}                                               // e
                                                // c
                                                // t

// Program Exit
// i
// o
// n

// Answer: defns.projection
```

Solution 28

```
void run() {
  {
    static S object_1("d", "w");                // d
    {
      S object_2("e", "m");                     // e
      {
        static S object_3("f", "o");            // f
        {
          static S object_4("n", "r");          // n
          S object_5("s", ".");                 // s
        }                                       // .
        static S object_6("a", "h");            // a
      }
```

```
      S object_7("r", "u");                                  // r
      static S object_8("g", "t");                           // g
    }                                                        // u
                                                             // m
    S object_9("e", "n");                                    // e
  }                                                          // n
  static S object_10("t", ".");                              // t
}

// Program Exit
// .
// t
// h
// r
// o
// w

// Answer: defns.argument.throw
```

Solution 29

```
void run() {
{
  }
  S object_1("c", "r");                                      // c
  S object_2("h", "a");                                      // h
}                                                            // a
                                                             // r

// Answer: char
```

Solution 30

```
void run() {
  S object_1("r", "p");                                      // r
  S object_2("a", "o");                                      // a
  S object_3("n", "r");                                      // n
  {
    S object_4("g", "e");                                    // g
  }                                                          // e
  {
    S object_5(".", "d");                                    // .
  }                                                          // d
```

```
}                                                   // r
                                                    // o
                                                    // p

// Answer: range.drop
```

Solution 31

```
void run() {
  S object_1("i", "e");                             // i
  S object_2("t", "g");                             // t
  S object_3("e", "n");                             // e
  S object_4("r", "a");                             // r
    {
  }
  S object_5("a", "r");                             // a
{
    {
      S object_6("t", "o");                         // t
    }                                               // o
    {
      S object_7("r", ".");                         // r
    }                                               // .
  }
}                                                   // r
                                                    // a
                                                    // n
                                                    // g
                                                    // e

// Answer: iterator.range
```

Solution 32

```
void run() {
  {
    S object_1("s", "t");                           // s
  }                                                 // t
  {
    S object_2("r", "n");                           // r
    {
      S object_3("i", ".");                         // i
        {
```

```
      }
      {
        S object_4("n", "g");                          // n
    }                                                  // g
      {
        S object_5("s", "t");                          // s
      }                                                // t
      S object_6("r", "m");                            // r
        {
      }
      S object_7("e", "a");                            // e
    }                                                  // a
                                                       // m
                                                       // .
    S object_8("g", "e");                              // g
    }                                                  // e
                                                       // n
    S object_9("e", "l");                              // e
  S object_10("r", "a");                               // r
}                                                      // a
                                                       // l

// Answer: stringstream.general
```

Solution 33

```
void run() {
  {
  }
  S *object_1 = new S("s", "e");                       // s
  delete object_1;                                     // e
  S *object_2 = nullptr;
  S *object_3 = new S("t", "t");                       // t
}

// Answer: set
```

Solution 34

```
void run() {
  {
    S *object_1 = nullptr;
  }
  S *object_2 = new S("b", "i");                    // b
  S *object_3 = nullptr;
  delete object_2;                                  // i
  object_3 = new S("t", "q");                       // t
  S *object_4 = nullptr;
}

// Answer: bit
```

Solution 35

```
void run() {
  S *object_1 = nullptr;
  S *object_2 = new S("f", "o");                    // f
  {
    S *object_3 = new S("l", "x");                  // l
  }
  delete object_2;                                  // o
  S *object_4 = nullptr;
  object_4 = new S("o", "r");                       // o
  S *object_5 = nullptr;
  delete object_4;                                  // r
  {
    S *object_6 = new S("l", "h");                  // l
  }
}

// Answer: floorl
```

Solution 36

```
void run() {
  {
    S *object_1 = nullptr;
    {
    }
    object_1 = new S("g", "w");                       // g
  }
  {
  }
  S *object_2 = nullptr;
  object_2 = new S("r", "a");                         // r
  delete object_2;                                    // a
  S *object_3 = nullptr;
  S *object_4 = new S("m", ".");                      // m
  S *object_5 = nullptr;
  delete object_4;                                    // .
  S *object_6 = new S("b", "a");                      // b
  delete object_6;                                    // a
  object_3 = new S("s", "x");                         // s
  object_5 = new S("i", "c");                         // i
  delete object_5;                                    // c
  S *object_7 = nullptr;
}

// Answer: gram.basic
```

Solution 37

```
void run() {
  S *object_1 = nullptr;
  S *object_2 = new S("r", "w");                      // r
  object_1 = new S("a", "h");                         // a
  {
    S *object_3 = new S("n", "d");                    // n
  }
  S *object_4 = new S("g", "r");                      // g
  {
    S *object_5 = new S("e", ".");                    // e
    delete object_5;                                  // .
  }
  S *object_6 = new S("s", "l");                      // s
```

```
  S *object_7 = nullptr;
  {
    S *object_8 = new S("p", "a");                    // p
  }
  delete object_6;                                    // l
  object_7 = new S("i", "t");                         // i
  delete object_7;                                    // t
  S *object_9 = nullptr;
}

// Answer: range.split
```

Solution 38

```
void run() {
  S *object_1 = nullptr;
  {
    {
      {
        S *object_2 = nullptr;
        object_2 = new S("r", "o");                   // r
        S *object_3 = nullptr;
      }
      object_1 = new S("e", "y");                     // e
      S *object_4 = new S("m", "k");                  // m
      S *object_5 = nullptr;
      S *object_6 = new S("q", "e");                  // q
      {
        object_5 = new S("u", "u");                   // u
        S *object_7 = nullptr;
        S *object_8 = new S("o", "x");                // o
      }
      S *object_9 = new S("f", "y");                  // f
    }
    S *object_10 = nullptr;
  }
}

// Answer: remquof
```

Solution 39

```
void run() {
  {
    S *object_1 = nullptr;
  }
  S *object_2 = new S("t", "w");                    // t
  S *object_3 = new S("i", "p");                    // i
  S *object_4 = nullptr;
  object_4 = new S("m", "h");                       // m
  S object_5("e", "d");                             // e
}                                                   // d

// Answer: timed
```

Solution 40

```
void run() {
  S *object_1 = nullptr;
  S *object_2 = new S("i", "s");                    // i
  S *object_3 = new S("o", "s");                    // o
  delete object_3;                                  // s
  S object_4(".", "n");                             // .
  {
    S *object_5 = nullptr;
    delete object_2;                                // s
    {
      S *object_6 = new S("y", "d");                // y
    }
  }
}                                                   // n

// Answer: ios.syn
```

Solution 41

```
void run() {
  S object_1("c", "t");                                  // c
  S *object_2 = new S("m", "p");                         // m
  S *object_3 = nullptr;
  delete object_2;                                       // p
  {
    object_3 = new S(".", "p");                          // .
  }
  S *object_4 = new S("c", "d");                         // c
  S *object_5 = new S("o", "e");                         // o
  S object_6("n", "p");                                  // n
  {
    S object_7("c", "e");                                // c
  }                                                      // e
}                                                        // p
                                                         // t

// Answer: cmp.concept
```

Solution 42

```
void run() {
  S *object_1 = new S("s", "t");                         // s
  S object_2("t", "e");                                  // t
  {
    S object_3("m", "i");                                // m
    {
      delete object_1;                                   // t
      {
      }
    }
    S *object_4 = new S(".", "i");                       // .
    S object_5("w", "h");                                // w
  }                                                      // h
                                                         // i
  S *object_6 = nullptr;
  S *object_7 = nullptr;
  S *object_8 = new S("l", "d");                         // l
}                                                        // e

// Answer: stmt.while
```

Solution 43

```
void run() {
  S *object_1 = new S("s", "i");                    // s
  S object_2("e", "w");                             // e
  S *object_3 = nullptr;
  {
    object_3 = new S("t", "v");                     // t
    S *object_4 = nullptr;
    S object_5(".", "o");                           // .
  }                                                 // o
  delete object_3;                                  // v
  S *object_6 = new S("e", "i");                    // e
  S object_7("r", "e");                             // r
  {
    S *object_8 = nullptr;
    {
      S object_9("v", "i");                         // v
    }                                               // i
  }
}                                                   // e
                                                    // w

// Answer: set.overview
```

Solution 44

```
void run() {
  S *object_1 = nullptr;
  {
    S object_2("r", "s");                           // r
    S *object_3 = new S("a", "g");                  // a
    object_1 = new S("n", "y");                     // n
    delete object_3;                                // g
    S *object_4 = new S("e", "p");                  // e
  }                                                 // s
  S *object_5 = new S(":", ":");                    // :
  {
    delete object_5;                                // :
    {
      S object_6("c", "g");                         // c
      S *object_7 = new S("r", "t");                // r
      S object_8("b", "e");                         // b
```

```
    }                                               // e
                                                    // g
  }
  {
    S *object_9 = new S("i", "v");                  // i
  }
  S *object_10 = new S("n", "i");                   // n
}

// Answer: ranges::crbegin
```

Solution 45

```
void run() {
  S *object_1 = new S("c", "o");                    // c
  {
    static S object_2("o", "e");                    // o
    S *object_3 = new S("r", "h");                  // r
  }
  delete object_1;                                  // o
  static S object_4("u", "n");                      // u
  static S object_5("t", "i");                      // t
}

// Program Exit
// i
// n
// e

// Answer: coroutine
```

Solution 46

```
void run() {
  S *object_1 = new S("r", "y");                    // r
  {
    static S object_2("a", "w");                    // a
  }
  {
    S *object_3 = new S("n", ".");                  // n
    static S object_4("g", "e");                    // g
    S *object_5 = new S("e", "s");                  // e
    delete object_3;                                // .
```

```
    static S object_6("v", "i");                 // v
  }
}

// Program Exit
// i
// e
// w

// Answer: range.view
```

Solution 47

```
void run() {
  static S object_1("o", "l"); S *object_2 = nullptr; // o
  static S object_3("p", "a");                   // p
  S *object_4 = new S("t", "f");                 // t
  {
    S *object_5 = nullptr;
    S *object_6 = new S("i", "l");               // i
    static S object_7("o", "n");                 // o
  }
}

// Program Exit
// n
// a
// l

// Answer: optional
```

Solution 48

```
void run() {
  static S object_1("s", "s");                   // s
  S *object_2 = nullptr;
  S *object_3 = new S("t", "r");                 // t
  {
    delete object_3;                             // r
  }
  S *object_4 = new S("i", "."); static S object_5("n", "p"); // i
                                                 // n
  S *object_6 = new S("g", "w");                 // g
```

```
  delete object_4;                               // .
  S *object_7 = nullptr;
  S *object_8 = new S("o", "p");                 // o
}

// Program Exit
// p
// s

// Answer: string.ops
```

Solution 49

```
void run() {
  S *object_1 = nullptr; object_1 = new S("i", "t"); // i
  static S object_2("n", "r");                   // n
  {
    S *object_3 = new S("s", ".");               // s
    {
      S *object_4 = nullptr;
      object_4 = new S("e", "a");                // e
      static S object_5("r", "o");               // r
      delete object_1;                           // t
      {
        delete object_3;                         // .
      }
      S *object_6 = nullptr;
      static S object_7("i", "t");               // i
      object_6 = new S("t", "i");                // t
      S *object_8 = new S("e", "r");             // e
      static S object_9("r", "a");               // r
    }
  }
}

// Program Exit
// a
// t
// o
// r

// Answer: insert.iterator
```

Solution 50

```
void run() {
  static S object_1("f", "n"); {                      // f
    {
      S *object_2 = nullptr;
    }
    S *object_3 = nullptr;
    S *object_4 = new S("u", "w");                     // u
  }
  {
    static S object_5("n", "f");                       // n
    static S object_6("c", "m");                       // c
    S *object_7 = nullptr; }
  {
    S *object_8 = new S(".", "n");                     // .
  }
  S *object_9 = nullptr;
  object_9 = new S("m", "w");                          // m
  S *object_10 = new S("e", "q");                      // e
}

// Program Exit
// m
// f
// n

// Answer: func.memfn
```

Solution 51

```
void run() {
S *object_1 = new S("f", "n");                         // f
  S *object_2 = new S("u", "i");                       // u
    delete object_1;                                   // n
  {
    static S object_3("c", "f");                       // c
    S *object_4 = new S(".", "k");                     // .
    static S object_5("d", "e");                       // d
  }
}

// Program Exit
```

```
// e
// f

// Answer: func.def
```

Solution 52

```
void run() {
  S *object_1 = nullptr;
  static S object_2("c", "g");                    // c
  S object_3("o", "i");                           // o
  {
    static S object_4("u", "n");                  // u
    S object_5("n", "t");                         // n
  }                                               // t
  S *object_6 = nullptr;
}                                                 // i

// Program Exit
// n
// g

// Answer: counting
```

Solution 53

```
void run() {
  {
  }
  S *object_1 = new S("b", "i");                  // b
  delete object_1;                                // i
  S object_2("n", "r");                           // n
  S *object_3 = new S("a", "r");                  // a
  {
    delete object_3;                              // r
  }
  S object_4("y", "a");                           // y
    static S object_5("_", "h");                  // _
  S *object_6 = new S("s", "i");                  // s
  static S object_7("e", "c");                    // e
}                                                 // a
                                                  // r
```

```
// Program Exit
// c
// h

// Answer: binary_search
```

Solution 54

```
void run() {
  S *object_1 = new S("s", "l");                 // s
  delete object_1;                                // l
S *object_2 = new S("i", "s");                   // i
  S object_3("c", "s");                           // c
  S *object_4 = new S("e", "r");                 // e
  {
    S *object_5 = nullptr;
  }
  S object_6(".", "e");                           // .
  S *object_7 = new S("a", "c");                 // a
  {
    delete object_7;                              // c
    {
      static S object_8("c", "s");                // c
    }
  }
}                                                 // e
                                                  // s

// Program Exit
// s

// Answer: slice.access
```

Solution 55

```
void run() {
  {
    {
    }
    static S object_1("i", "e");                        // i
    S object_2("n", "d");                               // n
  }                                                     // d
  S *object_3 = new S("e", "_");                        // e
  {
    static S object_4("x", "c");                        // x
    }
  delete object_3;                                      // _
  S *object_5 = nullptr;
  S *object_6 = new S("s", "e");                        // s
  object_5 = new S("e", "q");                           // e
  delete object_5;                                      // q
  S object_7("u", "n");                                 // u
  S *object_8 = nullptr;
  delete object_6;                                      // e
  S *object_9 = nullptr;
}                                                       // n

// Program Exit
// c
// e

// Answer: index_sequence
```

Solution 56

```
void run() {
  S *object_1 = new S("r", "i");                        // r
  S *object_2 = nullptr;
  object_2 = new S("e", "n");                           // e
  S object_3(".", "i");                                 // .
  S *object_4 = nullptr;
  S object_5("r", "s");                                 // r
  S *object_6 = new S("e", "o");                        // e
  static S object_7("s", "e");                          // s
  {
    S object_8("u", "t");                               // u
```

```
    static S object_9("l", "z");                    // l
  }                                                 // t
  S object_10("s", ".");                            // s
}                                                   // .
                                                    // s
                                                    // i

// Program Exit
// z
// e

// Answer: re.results.size
```

Solution 57

```
void run() {
  S *object_1 = new S("r", "j");                    // r
  S object_2("e", "n");                             // e
  S *object_3 = new S(".", "n");                    // .
  S object_4("s", "y");                             // s
  {
    S *object_5 = nullptr;
  }
}                                                   // y
                                                    // n

// Answer: re.syn
```

Solution 58

```
void run() {
  S *object_1 = nullptr;
  S *object_2 = new S("r", "e");                    // r
  {
    delete object_2;                                // e
  }
  object_1 = new S("m", "m");                       // m
  S *object_3 = nullptr;
  S *object_4 = new S("q", "i");                    // q
  S object_5("u", "o");                             // u
}                                                   // o

// Answer: remquo
```

Solution 59

```
void run() {
  S object_1("e", "s");                         // e
  {
  }
  static S object_2("x", "t");                  // x
  S object_3("p", "n");                         // p
  S *object_4 = new S("r", "j");                // r
  S *object_5 = new S(".", "u");                // .
  S object_6("c", "o");                         // c
}                                               // o
                                                // n
                                                // s

// Program Exit
// t

// Answer: expr.const
```

Solution 60

```
void run() {
  S *object_1 = new S("C", "o");                // C
  delete object_1;                              // o
  S object_2("n", "n");                         // n
  static S object_3("t", "r");                  // t
  {
    S *object_4 = new S("a", "q");              // a
    {
      S *object_5 = nullptr;
      static S object_6("i", "e");              // i
    }
  }
}                                               // n

// Program Exit
// e
// r

// Answer: Container
```

Solution 61

```
void run() {
  S *object_1 = nullptr;
  S *object_2 = new S("w", "x");                    // w
  object_1 = new S("m", "c");                       // m
  {
    S *object_3 = new S("e", "x");                  // e
  }
  S *object_4 = new S("m", "h");                    // m
  delete object_1;                                  // c
  S *object_5 = nullptr;
  {
    static S object_6("h", "r");                    // h
  }
}

// Program Exit
// r

// Answer: wmemchr
```

Solution 62

```
void run() {
  static S object_1("f", "t");                      // f
  {
    S *object_2 = new S("i", "a");                  // i
    static S object_3("n", "o");                    // n
    S object_4("d", "_");                           // d
    {
      static S object_5("_", "n");                  // _
    }
    S *object_6 = new S("i", "i");                  // i
    S *object_7 = new S("f", "r");                  // f
  }                                                 // _
}

// Program Exit
// n
// o
// t

// Answer: find_if_not
```

Solution 63

```
void run() {
  {
  }
  S *object_1 = nullptr;
  {
    S *object_2 = nullptr;
    S object_3("s", "r");                         // s
    object_1 = new S("u", "h");                   // u
    static S object_4("b", "t");                  // b
    S *object_5 = nullptr;
    static S object_6("t", "c");                  // t
  }                                               // r
  S *object_7 = new S("a", "m");                  // a
}

// Program Exit
// c
// t

// Answer: subtract
```

Solution 64

```
void run() {
  S *object_1 = nullptr;
  {
    object_1 = new S("t", "e");                   // t
    static S object_2("h", "q");                  // h
    S object_3("r", ".");                         // r
    {
      S *object_4 = nullptr;
      static S object_5("e", "e");                // e
      S *object_6 = new S("a", "s");              // a
    }
    static S object_7("d", "r");                  // d
  }                                               // .
}

// Program Exit
// r
// e
```

```
// q

// Answer: thread.req
```

Solution 65

```
void run() {
  static S object_1("d", "t");                              // d
  S object_2("c", "i");                                     // c
  {
    S *object_3 = nullptr;
    {
      static S object_4("l", "i");                          // l
      object_3 = new S(".", "e");                           // .
      S *object_5 = new S("c", "n");                        // c
      S *object_6 = nullptr;
      {
        static S object_7("o", "n");                        // o
        delete object_5;                                    // n
        object_6 = new S("s", "e");                         // s
        S *object_8 = new S("t", "k");                      // t
      }
    }
  }
}                                                           // i

// Program Exit
// n
// i
// t

// Answer: dcl.constinit
```

Solution 66

```
void run() {
  S *object_1 = nullptr;
  {
    S object_2("i", "o");                          // i
  }                                                // o
  static S object_3("s", "t");                     // s
  S object_4("_", "i");                            // _
  {
    object_1 = new S("b", "s");                    // b
    S object_5("a", "n");                          // a
    delete object_1;                               // s
    {
      S *object_6 = nullptr;
      S *object_7 = new S("e", ":");               // e
      delete object_7;                             // :
      object_6 = new S(":", "x");                  // :
      S *object_8 = new S("I", "k");               // I
    }
  }                                                // n
}                                                  // i

// Program Exit
// t

// Answer: ios_base::Init
```

Solution 67

```
void run() {
  S object_1("i", "t");                            // i
  static S object_2("n", "e");                     // n
  S *object_3 = nullptr;
  static S object_4("_", "p");                     // _
  S *object_5 = new S("p", "l");                   // p
  delete object_5;                                 // l
  S *object_6 = new S("a", "g");                   // a
  static S object_7("c", "y");                     // c
  S object_8("e", "_");                            // e
}                                                  // _
                                                   // t
```

```
// Program Exit
// y
// p
// e

// Answer: in_place_type
```

Solution 68

```
void run() {
  static S object_1("t", "o");              // t
  S *object_2 = nullptr;
  object_2 = new S("i", "r");               // i
  S *object_3 = nullptr;
  S object_4("m", "n");                     // m
  static S object_5("e", "i");              // e
  S *object_6 = new S(".", "u");            // .
  S object_7("d", "o");                     // d
  {
    delete object_6;                        // u
  }
  delete object_2;                          // r
  static S object_8("a", ".");              // a
  S object_9("t", "i");                     // t
}                                           // i
                                            // o
                                            // n

// Program Exit
// .
// i
// o

// Answer: time.duration.io
```

Solution 69

```
void run() {
  S object_1("r", "e");                                  // r
  {
    S object_2("a", "n");                                // a
  }                                                      // n
  S *object_3 = nullptr;
  {
    S object_4("g", "e");                                // g
    {
      S object_5("e", "s");                              // e
    }                                                    // s
    object_3 = new S(":", "s");                          // :
    S object_6(":", "m");                                // :
    S *object_7 = nullptr;
  }                                                      // m
                                                         // e
  S *object_8 = new S("r", "b");                         // r
  S *object_9 = new S("g", "o");                         // g
}                                                        // e

// Answer: ranges::merge
```

Solution 70

```
void run() {
  static S object_1("t", "l");                           // t
  S *object_2 = nullptr;
  object_2 = new S("i", ".");                            // i
  S *object_3 = new S("m", "a");                         // m
  S object_4("e", "e");                                  // e
  S *object_5 = new S(".", "t");                         // .
  S object_6("c", "n");                                  // c
  {
    static S object_7("a", "a");                         // a
    S object_8("l", "e");                                // l
    delete object_2;                                     // .
    static S object_9("g", "r");                         // g
  }                                                      // e
}                                                        // n
                                                         // e
```

```
// Program Exit
// r
// a
// l

// Answer: time.cal.general
```

Solution 71

```
void run() {
  {
    S object_1("c", "i");                          // c
    static S object_2("s", "l");                   // s
    S object_3("t", "d");                          // t
  }                                                // d
                                                   // i
  S *object_4 = nullptr;
  S *object_5 = new S("n", "g");                   // n
  {
    S *object_6 = new S("t", "o");                 // t
    {
      static S object_7(".", "a");                 // .
      {
        delete object_5;                           // g
        static S object_8("e", "r");               // e
        S *object_9 = nullptr;
        static S object_10("n", "e");              // n
      }
    }
  }
}

// Program Exit
// e
// r
// a
// l

// Answer: cstdint.general
```

Solution 72

```
void run() {
  {
    S *object_1 = new S("r", "r");                    // r
    static S object_2("a", "a");                      // a
  }
  S *object_3 = nullptr;
  static S object_4("n", "t");                        // n
  S *object_5 = new S("g", "i");                      // g
  object_3 = new S("e", ".");                         // e
  {
    S *object_6 = nullptr;
    delete object_3;                                  // .
  }
  S *object_7 = nullptr;
  static S object_8("p", "a");                        // p
  S object_9("r", "d");                               // r
  delete object_5;                                    // i
  object_7 = new S("m", "a");                         // m
  S object_10(".", "c");                              // .
}                                                     // c
                                                      // d

// Program Exit
// a
// t
// a

// Answer: range.prim.cdata
```

Solution 73

```
void run() {
  {
    thread_local S object_1("r", "n");                // r
  }
  thread_local S object_2("a", "i");                  // a
  thread_local S object_3("n", ":");                  // n
  thread_local S object_4("g", ":");                  // g
  thread_local S object_5("e", "s");                  // e
}
```

```
// Main Thread Exit
// s
// :
// :
// i
// n

// Answer: ranges::in
```

Solution 74

```
void run() {
  {
    thread_local S object_1("b", "g");            // b
    {
      thread_local S object_2("a", "n");          // a
    }
    thread_local S object_3("s", "i");            // s
  }
  thread_local S object_4("i", "r");              // i
  thread_local S object_5("c", "t");              // c
  thread_local S object_6("_", "s");              // _
}

// Main Thread Exit
// s
// t
// r
// i
// n
// g

// Answer: basic_string
```

Solution 75

```
void run() {
  {
    thread_local S object_1("r", "n");          // r
    {
      thread_local S object_2("a", "_");        // a
    }
    thread_local S object_3("n", "l");          // n
  }
  thread_local S object_4("g", "l");            // g
  thread_local S object_5("e", "i");            // e
  thread_local S object_6("s", "f");            // s
  thread_local S object_7(":", ":");            // :
}

// Main Thread Exit
// :
// f
// i
// l
// l
// _
// n

// Answer: ranges::fill_n
```

Solution 76

```
void run() {
  {
    thread_local S object_1("s", "y");          // s
  }
  {
    thread_local S object_2("t", "r");          // t
    {
      thread_local S object_3("a", "t");        // a
    }
    thread_local S object_4("c", "n");          // c
  }
  thread_local S object_5("k", "e");            // k
  thread_local S object_6("t", ".");            // t
  thread_local S object_7("r", "e");            // r
```

```
  thread_local S object_8("a", "c");                    // a
}

// Main Thread Exit
// c
// e
// .
// e
// n
// t
// r
// y

// Answer: stacktrace.entry
```

Solution 77

```
void run() {
  thread_local S object_1("c", "t");                    // c
  {
    thread_local S object_2("o", "_");                  // o
  }
  {
    thread_local S object_3("m", "e");                  // m
  }
  thread_local S object_4("m", "c");                    // m
  {
    thread_local S object_5("o", "n");                  // o
  }
  thread_local S object_6("n", "e");                    // n
  thread_local S object_7("_", "r");                    // _
  thread_local S object_8("r", "e");                    // r
  thread_local S object_9("e", "f");                    // e
}

// Main Thread Exit
// f
// e
// r
// e
// n
// c
// e
```

```
// _
// t

// Answer: common_reference_t
```

Solution 78

```
void run() {
  thread_local S object_1("s", "s");          // s
  {
    thread_local S object_2("t", "b");        // t
  }
  {
    thread_local S object_3("a", "o");        // a
  }
  thread_local S object_4("c", ".");          // c
  {
    thread_local S object_5("k", "c");        // k
    {
      thread_local S object_6("t", "i");      // t
    }
    thread_local S object_7("r", "s");        // r
  }
  thread_local S object_8("a", "a");          // a
  thread_local S object_9("c", "b");          // c
  thread_local S object_10("e", ".");         // e
}

// Main Thread Exit
// .
// b
// a
// s
// i
// c
// .
// o
// b
// s

// Answer: stacktrace.basic.obs
```

Solution 79

```
void run() {
  thread_local S object_1("t", "o");          // t
  static S object_2("i", "t");                // i
  {
    static S object_3("m", "n");              // m
  }
  static S object_4("e", "i");                // e
  thread_local S object_5(".", "p");          // .
}

// Main Thread Exit
// p
// o

// Program Exit
// i
// n
// t

// Answer: time.point
```

Solution 80

```
void run() {
  {
    thread_local S object_1("f", "u");        // f
  }
  {
    thread_local S object_2("s", "t");        // s
  }
  thread_local S object_3(".", "a");          // .
  thread_local S object_4("o", "t");          // o
  static S object_5("p", "s");                // p
  thread_local S object_6(".", "s");          // .
}

// Main Thread Exit
// s
// t
// a
// t
```

```
// u

// Program Exit
// s

// Answer: fs.op.status
```

Solution 81

```
void run() {
  static S object_1("c", "o");                        // c
  {
    thread_local S object_2("o", "l");                // o
    static S object_3("n", "t");                      // n
    {
      thread_local S object_4("v", "b");              // v
    }
    static S object_5("e", "_");                      // e
    thread_local S object_6("r", "i");                // r
    static S object_7("t", "e");                      // t
  }
}

// Main Thread Exit
// i
// b
// l

// Program Exit
// e
// _
// t
// o

// Answer: convertible_to
```

Solution 82

```
void run() {
  static S object_1("d", "s");                    // d
  {
    static S object_2("e", "n");                  // e
  }
  {
    thread_local S object_3("p", "e");            // p
    {
      static S object_4("r", "o");                // r
      thread_local S object_5(".", "v");          // .
    }
    static S object_6("c", "i");                  // c
  }
  static S object_7("o", "s");                    // o
  static S object_8("n", "r");                    // n
}

// Main Thread Exit
// v
// e

// Program Exit
// r
// s
// i
// o
// n
// s

// Answer: depr.conversions
```

Solution 83

```
void run() {
  thread_local S object_1("s", "e");              // s
  static S object_2("p", "s");                    // p
  thread_local S object_3("a", "m");              // a
  {
    static S object_4("n", "r");                  // n
    {
      thread_local S object_5("s", ".");          // s
```

```
    }
    static S object_6("t", "e");                          // t
    thread_local S object_7("r", "m");                    // r
    static S object_8("e", "b");                          // e
  }
  {
    static S object_9("a", "m");                          // a
  }
}

// Main Thread Exit
// m
// .
// m
// e

// Program Exit
// m
// b
// e
// r
// s

// Answer: spanstream.members
```

Solution 84

```
void run() {
  static S object_1("r", "r");                            // r
  {
    static S object_2("a", "o");                          // a
    thread_local S object_3("n", "a");                    // n
    {
      thread_local S object_4("g", "r");                  // g
    }
    {
      thread_local S object_5("e", "e");                  // e
      {
        thread_local S object_6(".", "t");                // .
      }
      thread_local S object_7("s", "i");                  // s
      static S object_8("p", "t");                        // p
      thread_local S object_9("l", ".");                  // l
```

```
    }
    thread_local S object_10("i", "t");                // i
  }
}

// Main Thread Exit
// t
// .
// i
// t
// e
// r
// a

// Program Exit
// t
// o
// r

// Answer: range.split.iterator
```

Solution 85

```
void run() {
  S object_1("f", "n");                                // f
  S object_2("e", "u"); {                              // e
    S object_3("s", "e");                              // s
  }                                                    // e
thread_local S object_4("t", "d");                     // t
  S object_5("r", "o");                                // r
}                                                      // o
                                                       // u
                                                       // n

// Main Thread Exit
// d

// Answer: fesetround
```

Solution 86

```
void run() {
  {
    thread_local S object_1("c", "d");                  // c
  }
  thread_local S object_2("l", "n");                    // l
  {
    thread_local S object_3("a", "e");                  // a
    S object_4("s", "s");                               // s
  }                                                     // s
  thread_local S object_5(".", "i");                    // .
  S object_6("f", "r");                                 // f
}                                                       // r

// Main Thread Exit
// i
// e
// n
// d

// Answer: class.friend
```

Solution 87

```
void run() {
  {
    {
        thread_local S object_1("s", "o"); }            // s
      thread_local S object_2("t", "i");                // t
    thread_local S object_3("r", "."); S object_4("i", "n"); // r
                                                        // i
  }                                                     // n
  thread_local S object_5("g", "w");                    // g
  S object_6(".", "e");                                 // .
  S object_7("v", "i");                                 // v
}                                                       // i
                                                        // e

// Main Thread Exit
// w
// .
// i
```

```
// o

// Answer: string.view.io
```

Solution 88

```
void run() {
  {
    thread_local S object_1("i", "s");          // i
    {
      S object_2("f", "e");                      // f
      { thread_local S object_3("s", "r");       // s
      } S object_4("t", "m");                    // t
      S object_5("r", ".");                      // r
      thread_local S object_6("e", "e");         // e
      S object_7("a", "m");                      // a
    }                                            // m
                                                 // .
                                                 // m
                                                 // e
    S object_8("m", "b");                        // m
  }                                              // b
}

// Main Thread Exit
// e
// r
// s

// Answer: ifstream.members
```

Solution 89

```
void run() {
  thread_local S object_1("c", "t"); thread_local S object_2("o", "s"); // c
                                                 // o
  {
    S object_3("u", "n"); }                      // u
                                                 // n
  thread_local S object_4("t", "n");             // t
  {
    S object_5("e", "e");                        // e
    { S object_6("d", "."); }                    // d
```

```
                                                      // .
    S object_7("i", "t");                             // i
  }                                                   // t
                                                      // e
thread_local S object_8("r", "o");                    // r
  thread_local S object_9(".", "c");                  // .
}

// Main Thread Exit
// c
// o
// n
// s
// t

// Answer: counted.iter.const
```

Solution 90

```
void run() {
  thread_local S object_1("s", "e");                  // s
  {
    S object_2("h", "u");                             // h
  }                                                   // u
  thread_local S object_3("f", "n");                  // f
  S object_4("f", "n");                               // f
  {
    S object_5("l", "e");                             // l
    { S object_6("e", "d");                           // e
      thread_local S object_7("_", "i");              // _
      S object_8("o", "r");                           // o
    }                                                 // r
                                                      // d
    thread_local S object_9("e", "g");                // e
    S object_10("r", "_");                            // r
  }                                                   // _
                                                      // e
}                                                     // n

// Main Thread Exit
// g
// i
// n
```

```
// e

// Answer: shuffle_order_engine
```

Solution 91

```
void run() {
  S *object_1 = nullptr;
  {
    S *object_2 = new S("m", "a");              // m
  }
  object_1 = new S("e", "m");                   // e
  delete object_1;                              // m
  S *object_3 = new S("_", "f");                // _
  delete object_3;                              // f
  S *object_4 = nullptr;
  thread_local S object_5("u", "n");            // u
}

// Main Thread Exit
// n

// Answer: mem_fun
```

Solution 92

```
void run() {
  S *object_1 = nullptr;
  {
    S *object_2 = nullptr;
  }
  object_1 = new S("s", "t");                   // s
  {
    delete object_1;                            // t
  }
  thread_local S object_3("r", "m");            // r
  S *object_4 = new S("s", "t");                // s
  S *object_5 = nullptr;
  delete object_4;                              // t
  object_5 = new S("r", "e");                   // r
  delete object_5;                              // e
  S *object_6 = new S("a", "l");                // a
}
```

```
// Main Thread Exit
// m

// Answer: strstream
```

Solution 93

```
void run() {
  {
    S *object_1 = nullptr;
    object_1 = new S("b", "i");                     // b
  }
  S *object_2 = new S("a", "t");                    // a
  {
    thread_local S object_3("d", "d");              // d
  }
  S *object_4 = nullptr;
  thread_local S object_5(".", "i");                // .
  delete object_2;                                  // t
  S *object_6 = new S("y", "e");                    // y
  object_4 = new S("p", "j");                       // p
  S *object_7 = new S("e", "h");                    // e
}

// Main Thread Exit
// i
// d

// Answer: bad.typeid
```

Solution 94

```
void run() {
  {
    thread_local S object_1("r", "g");              // r
    {
      thread_local S object_2("e", "a");            // e
    }
  }
  S *object_3 = nullptr;
  S *object_4 = new S(".", "m");                    // .
  delete object_4;                                  // m
```

```
  S *object_5 = nullptr;
  object_3 = new S("a", "s");                              // a
  thread_local S object_6("t", "l");                       // t
  S *object_7 = new S("c", "t");                           // c
  thread_local S object_8("h", "f");                       // h
}

// Main Thread Exit
// f
// l
// a
// g

// Answer: re.matchflag
```

Solution 95

```
void run() {
  {
    S *object_1 = nullptr;
    object_1 = new S("c", "a");                            // c
    S *object_2 = nullptr;
  }
  S *object_3 = new S("o", "u");                           // o
  S *object_4 = nullptr;
  delete object_3;                                         // u
  object_4 = new S("n", "i");                              // n
  {
    thread_local S object_5("t", "e");                     // t
    {
      S *object_6 = new S("l", "d");                       // l
      S *object_7 = nullptr;
      S *object_8 = new S("_", "s");                       // _
      thread_local S object_9("o", "n");                   // o
    }
  }
}

// Main Thread Exit
// n
// e

// Answer: countl_one
```

Solution 96

```
void run() {
  S *object_1 = nullptr;
  object_1 = new S("f", "s");                          // f
  delete object_1;                                     // s
  S *object_2 = new S(".", "n");                       // .
  S *object_3 = nullptr;
  thread_local S object_4("e", "t");                   // e
  {
    object_3 = new S("r", ".");                        // r
    S *object_5 = new S("r", "p");                     // r
  }
  delete object_3;                                     // .
  {
    S *object_6 = nullptr;
    S *object_7 = new S("r", "q");                     // r
    object_6 = new S("e", "p");                        // e
    {
      {
      }
      S *object_8 = nullptr;
      delete object_6;                                 // p
      thread_local S object_9("o", "r");               // o
    }
    S *object_10 = nullptr;
  }
}

// Main Thread Exit
// r
// t

// Answer: fs.err.report
```

Solution 97

```
void run() {
  thread_local S object_1("u", "t");               // u
  S *object_2 = nullptr;
  thread_local S object_3("i", "_");               // i
  S object_4("n", "2");                            // n
  object_2 = new S("t", "o");                      // t
  S *object_5 = new S("3", "g");                   // 3
}                                                  // 2

// Main Thread Exit
// _
// t

// Answer: uint32_t
```

Solution 98

```
void run() {
  {
    S *object_1 = nullptr;
    thread_local S object_2("w", "b");             // w
    object_1 = new S("c", "x");                    // c
    S *object_3 = nullptr;
    thread_local S object_4("t", "m");             // t
    S *object_5 = nullptr;
    S *object_6 = new S("o", "j");                 // o
  }
}

// Main Thread Exit
// m
// b

// Answer: wctomb
```

Solution 99

```
void run() {
  S *object_1 = nullptr;
  S object_2("t", "i");                          // t
  thread_local S object_3("e", "s");             // e
  object_1 = new S("m", "a");                    // m
  S object_4("p", "l");                          // p
  {
    thread_local S object_5(".", "a");           // .
  }
  S *object_6 = new S("a", "p");                 // a
  S *object_7 = nullptr;
}                                                // l
                                                 // i

// Main Thread Exit
// a
// s

// Answer: temp.alias
```

Solution 100

```
void run() {
  {
    {
      thread_local S object_1("s", "f");         // s
      {
        S *object_2 = nullptr;
        S *object_3 = new S("t", "s");           // t
        object_2 = new S("r", "d");              // r
        delete object_3;                         // s
      }
      S *object_4 = nullptr;
      thread_local S object_5("t", "u");         // t
      S object_6("r", "m");                      // r
      thread_local S object_7("e", "b");         // e
      S *object_8 = new S("a", "i");             // a
    }                                            // m
  }
}
```

```
// Main Thread Exit
// b
// u
// f

// Answer: strstreambuf
```

Solution 101

```
void run() {
  thread_local S object_1("c", "d");                 // c
  {
    S *object_2 = new S("f", "b");                   // f
    {
      thread_local S object_3("e", "a");             // e
      {
        S *object_4 = nullptr;
        S *object_5 = new S("n", "u");               // n
      }
      S *object_6 = new S("v", "v");                 // v
    }
    S object_7(".", "e");                            // .
    S *object_8 = new S("t", "q");                   // t
    S object_9("h", "r");                            // h
  }                                                  // r
                                                     // e
}

// Main Thread Exit
// a
// d

// Answer: cfenv.thread
```

Solution 102

```
void run() {
  {
    thread_local S object_1("c", "d");          // c
    S *object_2 = nullptr;
  }
  S *object_3 = new S("o", "c");                // o
  S *object_4 = nullptr;
  S *object_5 = new S("p", "h");                // p
  {
    S object_6("y", "_");                       // y
  }                                             // _
  S *object_7 = new S("b", "d");                // b
  S object_8("a", "r");                         // a
  {
    delete object_3;                            // c
    S object_9("k", "a");                       // k
    S *object_10 = new S("w", "p");             // w
  }                                             // a
}                                               // r

// Main Thread Exit
// d

// Answer: copy_backward
```

Solution 103

```
void run() {
  {
  }
  S *object_1 = nullptr;
  object_1 = new S("b", "i");                   // b
  delete object_1;                              // i
  thread_local S object_2("n", "d");            // n
  S *object_3 = new S("d", "r");                // d
  S object_4("e", "n");                         // e
  delete object_3;                              // r
  S *object_5 = new S("2", "y");                // 2
}                                               // n

// Main Thread Exit
```

```
// d

// Answer: binder2nd
```

Solution 104

```
void run() {
  {
    {
      S *object_1 = nullptr;
      thread_local S object_2("s", "d");          // s
      S *object_3 = nullptr;
      object_1 = new S("t", "t");                 // t
      S *object_4 = nullptr;
      S object_5("r", "o");                       // r
      thread_local S object_6("t", "l");          // t
    }                                             // o
  }
}

// Main Thread Exit
// l
// d

// Answer: strtold
```

Solution 105

```
void run() {
  {
    S object_1("i", "i");                         // i
    S *object_2 = new S("d", "e");                // d
    {
      S *object_3 = nullptr;
    }
    delete object_2;                              // e
    thread_local S object_4("n", "y");            // n
    S *object_5 = nullptr;
    thread_local S object_6("t", "t");            // t
    S *object_7 = nullptr;
  }                                               // i
}
```

```
// Main Thread Exit
// t
// y

// Answer: identity
```

Solution 106

```
void run() {
  S object_1("m", "l");                              // m
  thread_local S object_2("e", "c");                 // e
  S *object_3 = new S("m", ".");                     // m
  S object_4(".", "b");                              // .
  {
    S *object_5 = new S("r", "p");                   // r
  }
  {
    S *object_6 = new S("e", "k");                   // e
  }
  S object_7("s", "u");                              // s
  delete object_3;                                   // .
  {
    thread_local S object_8("p", "i");               // p
  }
}                                                    // u
                                                     // b
                                                     // l

// Main Thread Exit
// i
// c

// Answer: mem.res.public
```

Solution 107

```
void run() {
  S *object_1 = new S("a", "u");                    // a
  S *object_2 = nullptr;
  S object_3("l", "c");                             // l
  S *object_4 = nullptr;
  S *object_5 = new S("g", "x");                    // g
  {
    S object_6(".", "r");                           // .
    {
      thread_local S object_7("s", "h");            // s
      {
        S *object_8 = nullptr;
        object_2 = new S("e", "n");                 // e
      }
      S *object_9 = new S("a", "k");                // a
    }
  }                                                 // r
}                                                   // c

// Main Thread Exit
// h

// Answer: alg.search
```

Solution 108

```
void run() {
  thread_local S object_1("s", "l");                // s
  S *object_2 = nullptr;
  S object_3("t", "e");                             // t
  {
  }
  object_2 = new S("a", "c");                       // a
  {
    S *object_4 = nullptr;
    {
      delete object_2;                              // c
    }
    object_4 = new S("k", "q");                     // k
    thread_local S object_5("t", "a");              // t
    S object_6("r", ".");                           // r
```

```
    {
      thread_local S object_7("a", "r");          // a
    }
    S object_8("c", "e");                          // c
  }                                                // e
                                                   // .

  S *object_9 = nullptr;
  object_9 = new S("g", "f");                      // g
  S object_10("e", "n");                           // e
}                                                  // n
                                                   // e

// Main Thread Exit
// r
// a
// l

// Answer: stacktrace.general
```

Solution 109

```
void run() {
  S *object_1 = new S("c", "s");                   // c
  S *object_2 = nullptr;
  S *object_3 = new S("o", "w");                   // o
  S *object_4 = nullptr;
  object_4 = new S("d", "y");                      // d
  {
    S *object_5 = new S("e", "g"); thread_local S object_6("c", "e"); // e
                                                   // c
  }
  S *object_7 = new S("v", "h");                   // v
  {
    S("t", "_");                                   // t
                                                   // _
    S *object_9 = new S("b", "u");                 // b
    S object_10("a", "s");                         // a
  }                                                // s
}

// Main Thread Exit
// e
```

```
// Answer: codecvt_base
```

Solution 110

```
void run() {
  S object_1("f", ".");                          // f
  S *object_2 = new S("s", "y");                 // s
  S object_3(".", "m");                          // .
  S *object_4 = new S("f", "e");                 // f
  S *object_5 = nullptr;
  S object_6("i", "e");                          // i
  S *object_7 = nullptr;
  static S object_8("l", "n");                   // l
  {
    delete object_4;                             // e
  }
  static S object_9("s", "y");                   // s
  delete object_2;                               // y
  S *object_10 = new S("s", "f");                // s
  thread_local S object_11("t", "s");            // t
}                                                // e
                                                 // m
                                                 // .

// Main Thread Exit
// s

// Program Exit
// y
// n

// Answer: fs.filesystem.syn
```

Solution 111

```
void run() {
  static S object_1("t", "e");                    // t
  thread_local S object_2("h", "d");              // h
  thread_local S object_3("r", "n");              // r
  new S("e", "x");                                // e
  thread_local S object_5("a", "a");              // a
  S *object_6 = nullptr;
  thread_local S object_7("d", "h"); S *object_8 = new S(":", "i"); // d
                                                  // :

  {
    S object_9(":", "e");                         // :
    static S object_10("n", "l");                 // n
    object_6 = new S("a", "b");                   // a
    thread_local S object_11("t", "_");           // t
    S("i", "v");                                  // i
                                                  // v
  }                                               // e
}

// Main Thread Exit
// _
// h
// a
// n
// d

// Program Exit
// l
// e

// Answer: thread::native_handle
```

Solution 112

```
void run() {
  static S object_1("d", "e");                               // d
  S object_2("e", "i");                                      // e
  thread_local S object_3("f", "t");                         // f
  {
    thread_local S object_4("n", ".");                       // n
    S *object_5 = new S("s", "y");                           // s
    new S(".", "u");                                         // .
    thread_local S object_7("d", "c");                       // d
    {
      delete object_5;                                       // y
    }
    S *object_8 = nullptr;
    {
      S *object_9 = nullptr;
      {
        static S object_10("n", "p");                        // n
        S *object_11 = nullptr;
        static S object_12("a", "y");                        // a
        S *object_13 = new S("m", "r");                      // m
      }
    }
  }
}                                                            // i

// Main Thread Exit
// c
// .
// t

// Program Exit
// y
// p
// e

// Answer: defns.dynamic.type
```

Solution 113

```
void run() {
  static S object_1("d", "d");                     // d
  S *object_2 = nullptr;
  S *object_3 = new S("e", "i");                   // e
  static S object_4("r", "i");                     // r
  delete object_3;                                 // i
  delete new S("v", "e");                          // v
                                                   // e
  {
    new S("d", "y");                               // d
    S object_7(" ", "f");                          //
    object_2 = new S("t", "y");                    // t
    delete object_2;                               // y
    S *object_8 = nullptr;
    S *object_9 = new S("p", "e");                 // p
    delete object_9;                               // e
    static S object_10(" ", "e");                  //
  }                                                // f
  S object_11("o", "p");                           // o
  S *object_12 = nullptr;
  S("r", " ");                                     // r
                                                   //
  S object_14("t", "y");                           // t
}                                                  // y
                                                   // p

// Program Exit
// e
// i
// d

// Answer: derived type for typeid
```

Solution 114

```
void run() {
  new S("t", "f");                                 // t
  {
    S object_2("i", "l");                          // i
    {
      S *object_3 = new S("m", "p");               // m
      S object_4("e", ".");                        // e
    }                                              // .
    thread_local S object_5("c", "r");             // c
    static S object_6("a", "s");                   // a
  }                                                // l
  S *object_7 = nullptr;
  thread_local S object_8(".", "e");               // .
  object_7 = new S("m", "o");                      // m
  delete object_7;                                 // o
  S object_9("n", "b");                            // n
  {
    S *object_10 = new S("t", "q");                // t
    S object_11("h", ".");                         // h
  }                                                // .
  S *object_12 = nullptr;
  object_12 = new S("m", "x");                     // m
  S("e", "m");                                     // e
                                                   // m
  S *object_14 = nullptr;
  {
    S *object_15 = nullptr;
  }
}                                                  // b

// Main Thread Exit
// e
// r

// Program Exit
// s

// Answer: time.cal.month.members
```

Solution 115

```
void run() {
  S *object_1 = new S("s", "r");                          // s
  thread_local S object_2("y", "m"); static S object_3("s", "s"); // y
                                                          // s
    thread_local S object_4("e", "e");                    // e
  {
    thread_local S object_5("r", "m");                    // r
    S *object_6 = nullptr;
    thread_local S object_7("r", "n");                    // r
    S *object_8 = new S(".", "v");                        // .
    thread_local S object_9("e", "o");                    // e
  }
  S *object_10 = nullptr;
  delete object_1;                                        // r
  S *object_11 = new S("r", "h");                         // r
  static S object_12("c", "r");                           // c
  S *object_13 = new S("o", "d");                         // o
  static S object_14("n", "e");                           // n
  delete object_13;                                       // d
  {
    S object_15("i", "t");                                // i
  }                                                       // t
  S object_16("i", "n");                                  // i
  {
    S object_17("o", ".");                                // o
    static S object_18("n", "b");                         // n
  }                                                       // .
}                                                         // n

// Main Thread Exit
// o
// n
// m
// e
// m

// Program Exit
// b
// e
// r
// s
```

```
// Answer: syserr.errcondition.nonmembers
```

Solution 116

```
void run() {
  thread_local S object_1("t", "v");                  // t
  {
    static S object_2("e", "w");                      // e
    S *object_3 = new S("m", "r");                    // m
    S *object_4 = nullptr;
    S object_5("p", "a");                             // p
    S *object_6 = nullptr;
    object_6 = new S("l", "v");                       // l
  }                                                   // a
  S object_7("t", "o"); static S object_8("e", "e"); // t
                                                      // e
  {
    thread_local S object_9(".", "r");                // .
    thread_local S object_10("g", "e");               // g
  }
  S *object_11 = new S("s", "i");                     // s
  thread_local S object_12("l", "v");                 // l
  {
    S("i", "c");                                      // i
                                                      // c
  }
  S object_14("e", ".");                              // e
    S *object_15 = new S(".", "m");                   // .
  {
    S *object_16 = new S("a", "t");                   // a
    {
      S *object_17 = nullptr;
    }
    static S object_18("r", "i");                     // r
    {
      S object_19("r", "y");                          // r
      S *object_20 = new S("a", "h");                 // a
    }                                                 // y
  }
}                                                     // .
                                                      // o
```

```
// Main Thread Exit
// v
// e
// r
// v

// Program Exit
// i
// e
// w

// Answer: template.gslice.array.overview
```

Solution 117

```
void run() {
  S *object_1 = new S("i", "i");                    // i
  S *object_2 = nullptr;
  {
    thread_local S object_3("s", "l");              // s
  }
  S object_4("_", "t");                             // _
  S *object_5 = nullptr;
  S *object_6 = new S("t", "j");                    // t
  S object_7("r", "c");                             // r
  S *object_8 = nullptr;
  object_8 = new S("i", "w");                       // i
  static S object_9("v", "v");                      // v
  S *object_10 = nullptr;
  S *object_11 = nullptr;
  new S("i", "v");                                  // i
  static S object_13("a", "_");                     // a
  object_2 = new S("l", "f");                       // l
  {
    S object_14("l", "e");                          // l
    object_5 = new S("y", "v");                     // y
  S object_15("_", "d");                            // _
  }                                                 // d
                                                    // e
  S("f", "a");                                      // f
                                                    // a
  thread_local S object_17("u", "b");               // u
  S object_18("l", "u");                            // l
```

```
  object_11 = new S("t", "a");                          // t
  {
    static S object_19("_", "e");                       // _
    object_10 = new S("c", "t");                        // c
    S object_20("o", "r");                              // o
    S *object_21 = new S("n", "t");                     // n
    thread_local S object_22("s", "i");                 // s
    S *object_23 = new S("t", "k");                     // t
  }                                                     // r
}                                                       // u
                                                        // c
                                                        // t

// Main Thread Exit
// i
// b
// l

// Program Exit
// e
// _
// v

// Answer: is_trivially_default_constructible_v
```

Solution 118

```
void run() {
  S object_1("t", "_");                                 // t
  { thread_local S object_2("y", "r");                  // y
    S *object_3 = nullptr;
    S *object_4 = new S("p", "r");                      // p
    static S object_5("e", "r");                        // e
    S object_6(" ", "o");                               //
  }                                                     // o
  {
    static S object_7("f", "o");                        // f
    delete new S(" ", "u");                             //
                                                        // u
    S object_9("n", "d");                               // n
    {
      static S object_10("o", "t");                     // o
    }
```

```
    S *object_11 = nullptr;
    S *object_12 = new S("r", "b");                         // r
  }                                                         // d
  thread_local S object_13("e", "e");                       // e
  S("r", "e");                                              // r
                                                            // e

  {
    S object_15("d", "_");                                  // d
  }                                                         // _
{
    delete new S("m", "u");                                 // m
                                                            // u
    S *object_17 = new S("l", "t");                         // l
    S *object_18 = nullptr;
    {
      delete object_17;                                     // t
    }
    {
      new S("i", "v");                                      // i
      thread_local S object_20("s", "t");                   // s
    }
    S("e", "t");                                            // e
                                                            // t
    S object_22(":", "l");                                  // :
    thread_local S object_23(":", "i");                     // :
    {
      object_18 = new S("l", "a");                          // l
      static S object_24("o", "a");                         // o
      S("c", "a");                                          // c
                                                            // a

    }
  }                                                         // l
}                                                           // _

// Main Thread Exit
// i
// t
// e
// r

// Program Exit
// a
// t
```

```
// o
// r

// Answer: type of unordered_multiset::local_iterator
```

Solution 119

```
void run() {
    S *object_1 = new S("v", "l");                    // v
  thread_local S object_2("a", "a");                  // a
  S *object_3 = nullptr;
  {
    S *object_4 = nullptr;
    delete object_1;                                  // l
    {
      object_4 = new S("u", "t");                     // u
      static S object_5("e", "s");                    // e
      S *object_6 = new S("s", "_");                  // s
      {
        S object_7(" ", " ");                         //
        S *object_8 = new S("o", "r");                // o
        object_3 = new S("f", "A");                   // f
      }                                               //
      S *object_9 = new S("v", "O");                  // v
      S *object_10 = nullptr;
      {
        thread_local S object_11("a", "m");           // a
        {
          static S object_12("r", "o");               // r
          delete new S("i", "o");                     // i
                                                      // o
          S object_14("u", "T");                      // u
          object_10 = new S("s", "C");                // s
          new S(" ", "j");                            //
          delete object_3;                            // A
        }                                             // T
        S object_16("O", ".");                        // O
        new S("M", "f");                              // M
        thread_local S object_18("I", " ");           // I
        S *object_19 = new S("C", ".");               // C
        S *object_20 = nullptr;
        delete object_6;                              // _
        {
```

```
          static S object_21(".", "r");            // .
        }
        S *object_22 = nullptr;
        delete object_19;                          // .
      }                                            // .
      S("_", "L");                                 // _
                                                   // L
      {
        delete object_9;                           // O
        delete object_10;                          // C
        S *object_24 = nullptr;
      } S *object_25 = new S("K", "y");            // K
    }
    S object_26("_", "E");                         // _
    static S object_27("F", "c");                  // F
    thread_local S object_28("R", "E");            // R
  }                                                // E
}

// Main Thread Exit
// E
//
// m
// a

// Program Exit
// c
// r
// o
// s

// Answer: values of various ATOMIC_..._LOCK_FREE macros
```

Solution 120

```
void run() {
  thread_local S object_1("A", "b"); S *object_2 = new S(" ", "b"); // A
                                                        //
  thread_local S object_3("c", "a");                    // c
  delete new S("a", "l");                               // a
                                                        // l
  {
    static S object_5("l", ".");                        // l
  }
  delete new S("a", "b");                               // a
                                                        // b
  S("l", "e");                                          // l
                                                        // e
  S *object_8 = nullptr;
  static S object_9(" ", "e");                          //
  S *object_10 = new S("o", " ");                       // o
  delete object_2;                                      // b
  thread_local S object_11("j", "l");                   // j
  static S object_12("e", "p");                         // e
  S *object_13 = nullptr;
  thread_local S object_14("c", "l");                   // c
  static S object_15("t", "y");                         // t
  object_13 = new S(" ", "i"); delete object_13;        //
                                                        // i
  S *object_16 = new S("s", "v");                       // s
  delete object_10;                                     //
  S("a", "n");                                          // a
                                                        // n
  S *object_18 = nullptr;
  S *object_19 = new S(" ", "o");                       //
  object_18 = new S("o", "t");                          // o
  S *object_20 = new S("b", "w");                       // b
  S *object_21 = nullptr;
static S object_22("j", "t");                           // j
  static S object_23("e", " "); S object_24("c", "a"); // e
                                                        // c
  S object_25("t", "c");                                // t
  static S object_26(" ", "e");                         //
  S object_27("o", " ");                                // o
S *object_28 = new S("f", "d");                         // f
  new S(" ", "n");                                      //
```

```
  static S object_30("a", "l");                   // a
}                                                 //
                                                  // c
                                                  // a


// Main Thread Exit
// l
// l
// a
// b

// Program Exit
// l
// e
//
// t
// y
// p
// e
// .

// Answer: A callable object is an object of a callable type.
```

Solution 121

```
void run() {
  S object_1("s", "e");                           // s
  S *object_2 = new S("y", "a");                  // y
  {
    S *object_3 = nullptr;
  }
  static S object_4("n", "w");                    // n
  S object_5("c", "v");                           // c
  S *object_6 = new S("s", "y");                  // s
  {
    S object_7("t", "o");                         // t
    delete new S("r", "e");                       // r
                                                  // e
    S("a", "m");                                  // a
                                                  // m
    S *object_10 = nullptr;
    static S object_11(".", "e");                 // .
    thread_local S object_12("o", "v");           // o
```

```
    delete new S("s", "y");                          // s
                                                     // y
    {
      object_10 = new S("n", "i");                   // n
      {
        S object_14("c", "s");                       // c
      }                                              // s
      new S("t", "d");                               // t
      static S object_16("r", "i");                  // r
    }
    {
      thread_local S object_17("e", "r");            // e
    }
    delete object_2;                                 // a
    S object_18("m", ".");                           // m
  }                                                  // .
                                                     // o
}                                                    // v
                                                     // e

// Main Thread Exit
// r
// v

// Program Exit
// i
// e
// w

// Answer: syncstream.osyncstream.overview
```

Solution 122

```
void run() {
  S *object_1 = nullptr;
  thread_local S object_2("s", "a");                 // s
  {
    S object_3("o", "_");                            // o
    {
      S *object_4 = new S("u", "c");                 // u
      S object_5("r", "n");                          // r
      {
        delete object_4;                             // c
```

```
        S *object_6 = new S("e", "n");              // e
        {
          S("_", "l");                              // _
                                                    // l
        }
        {
          S *object_8 = new S("o", "i");            // o
        }
        S object_9("c", "o");                       // c
        thread_local S object_10("a", "n");         // a
        delete new S("t", "i");                     // t
                                                    // i
        {
          S *object_12 = new S("o", "p");           // o
          {
            static S object_13("n", "e");           // n
            S *object_14 = nullptr;
            S(":", ":");                            // :
                                                    // :
            delete new S("f", "u");                 // f
                                                    // u
            delete object_6;                        // n
            S *object_17 = new S("c", "d");         // c
            static S object_18("t", "m");           // t
            S *object_19 = new S("i", "n");         // i
          }
          {
            S *object_20 = nullptr;
          }
        }
      }                                             // o
    }                                               // n
  }                                                 // _
}

// Main Thread Exit
// n
// a

// Program Exit
// m
// e
```

```
// Answer: source_location::function_name
```

Solution 123

```
void run() {
  S("t", "y");                                    // t
                                                  // y
  S *object_2 = nullptr;
  thread_local S object_3("p", "t");              // p
  S *object_4 = new S("e", "o");                  // e
  object_2 = new S(" ", "n");                     //
  delete object_4;                                // o
  S *object_5 = nullptr;
  static S object_6("f", "e");                    // f
  S *object_7 = new S(" ", "m");                  //
  thread_local S object_8("u", "_");              // u
  delete object_2;                                // n
  thread_local S object_9("o", "e");              // o
  S *object_10 = nullptr;
  object_5 = new S("r", "e");                     // r
  thread_local S object_11("d", "c");             // d
  delete new S("e", "r");                         // e
                                                  // r
  delete object_5;                                // e
  S *object_13 = nullptr;
  S("d", "_");                                    // d
                                                  // _
  delete object_7;                                // m
  new S("a", "y");                                // a
  object_13 = new S("p", ":");                    // p
  delete object_13;                               // :
  S *object_16 = new S(":", "e");                 // :
  thread_local S object_17("d", "n");             // d
  {
    object_10 = new S("i", "f");                  // i
  }
  {
    {
      S *object_18 = nullptr;
      delete object_10;                           // f
    }
    static S object_19("f", "p");                 // f
    {
```

```
      static S object_20("e", "y");                   // e
    }
    delete new S("r", "e");                           // r
                                                      // e
  }
}

// Main Thread Exit
// n
// c
// e
// _
// t

// Program Exit
// y
// p
// e

// Answer: type of unordered_map::difference_type
```

Solution 124

```
void run() {
  static S object_1("u", "o");                        // u
  static S object_2("n", "r");                        // n
  S *object_3 = nullptr;
  S *object_4 = new S("i", "f");                      // i
  static S object_5("t", "c");                        // t
  S object_6(" ", " ");                               //
  S("s", "u");                                        // s
                                                      // u
  S *object_8 = nullptr;
  delete object_4;                                    // f
  {
    object_3 = new S("f", "t");                       // f
    S object_9("i", "o");                             // i
    static S object_10("x", "i");                     // x
    thread_local S object_11(" ", "s");               //
    S *object_12 = new S("w", "p");                   // w
    static S object_13("h", "m");                     // h
    {
      object_8 = new S("e", "s");                     // e
```

```
    }
    thread_local S object_14("n", "i");              // n
    S *object_15 = new S(" ", "k");                  //
    S object_16("P", "i");                           // P
    S *object_17 = nullptr;
    {
      S *object_18 = nullptr;
    }
    S("e", "r");                                     // e
                                                     // r
  }                                                  // i
                                                     // o
  S object_20("d", "e");                             // d
  static S object_21(":", " ");                      // :
  S object_22(":", "p");                             // :
  delete new S("t", "y");                            // t
                                                     // y
}                                                    // p
                                                     // e
                                                     //

// Main Thread Exit
// i
// s

// Program Exit
//
// m
// i
// c
// r
// o

// Answer: unit suffix when Period::type is micro
```

Solution 125

```
void run() {
  S *object_1 = new S("a", "n");                   // a
  S object_2("l", "o");                            // l
  {
    S("i", "g");                                   // i
                                                   // g
  }
  S *object_4 = nullptr;
  delete object_1;                                 // n
  static S object_5("m", "t");                     // m
  S object_6("e", " ");                            // e
  object_4 = new S("n", "f");                      // n
  S object_7("t", "s");                            // t
  static S object_8(" ", "c");                     //
  S object_9("o", "s");                            // o
  delete object_4;                                 // f
  {
    S *object_10 = new S(" ", "f");                //
    S object_11("b", "t");                         // b
    static S object_12("i", "e");                  // i
  }                                                // t
  delete new S("-", "f");                          // -
                                                   // f
  new S("i", "i");                                 // i
  S *object_15 = new S("e", " ");                  // e
  {
    S("l", "d");                                   // l
                                                   // d
    S *object_17 = new S("s", "w");                // s
  }
  delete object_15;                                //
  S("w", "i");                                     // w
                                                   // i
  S *object_19 = new S("t", "i");                  // t
  thread_local S object_20("h", "b");              // h
  delete object_19;                                // i
  new S("n", "r");                                 // n
  S object_22(" ", "a");                           //
  {
  }
  static S object_23("a", "j");                    // a
```

```
  {
    S *object_24 = new S(" ", "a");                    //
  }
  S object_25("c", "l");                               // c
}                                                      // l
                                                       // a
                                                       // s
                                                       // s
                                                       //
                                                       // o

// Main Thread Exit
// b

// Program Exit
// j
// e
// c
// t

// Answer: alignment of bit-fields within a class object
```

Solution 126

```
void run() {
  delete new S("d", "e");                              // d
                                                       // e
  {
    {
      S *object_2 = new S("f", "x");                   // f
      S("a", "u");                                     // a
                                                       // u
      thread_local S object_4("l", "l");               // l
      static S object_5("t", "t");                     // t
    }
    {
      S *object_6 = new S(" ", "i");                   //
    }
    delete new S("n", "u");                            // n
                                                       // u
  }
  static S object_8("m", "e");                         // m
  {
```

```
  }
  new S("b", "k");                                    // b
  static S object_10("e", "s");                       // e
  S *object_11 = new S("r", "f");                     // r
  S object_12(" ", "m");                              //
  new S("o", "x");                                    // o
  delete object_11;                                   // f
  static S object_14(" ", "i");                       //
  S object_15("b", "_");                              // b
  {
    S object_16("u", "c");                            // u
  }                                                   // c
  S("k", "e");                                        // k
                                                      // e
  S *object_18 = new S("t", "s");                     // t
  delete object_18;                                   // s
  S *object_19 = nullptr;
  {
    static S object_20(" ", "t");                     //
    S object_21("i", "r");                            // i
    thread_local S object_22("n", "u");               // n
    {
      object_19 = new S(" ", "o");                    //
      delete new S("u", "n");                         // u
                                                      // n
      delete object_19;                               // o
    }
    S *object_24 = nullptr;
  }                                                   // r
  S("d", "e");                                        // d
                                                      // e
  new S("r", "p");                                    // r
  S object_27("e", "d");                              // e
}                                                     // d
                                                      // _
                                                      // m

// Main Thread Exit
// u
// l

// Program Exit
// t
```

```
// i
// s
// e
// t

// Answer: default number of buckets in unordered_multiset
```

Solution 127

```
void run() {
  thread_local S object_1("r", "w");                // r
  {
    S *object_2 = new S("e", "a");                   // e
  }
  S object_3("t", "c");                              // t
  new S("u", "t");                                   // u
  {
    S *object_5 = new S("r", " ");                   // r
    new S("n", "w");                                 // n
    {
      delete object_5;                               //
      S *object_7 = nullptr;
      {
        thread_local S object_8("v", ":");           // v
        S object_9("a", " ");                        // a
        S *object_10 = nullptr;
        static S object_11("l", "t");                // l
        S object_12("u", "e");                       // u
      }                                              // e
                                                     //
      thread_local S object_13("o", ":");            // o
      S *object_14 = new S("f", " ");                // f
      delete object_14;                              //
      thread_local S object_15("b", "s");            // b
      S object_16("a", "o");                         // a
      S *object_17 = nullptr;
      thread_local S object_18("d", "s");            // d
      object_7 = new S("_", "n");                    // _
    }                                                // o
    {
      static S object_19("p", "a");                  // p
      thread_local S object_20("t", "e");            // t
      S *object_21 = nullptr;
```

```
    }
    S *object_22 = new S("i", "o");                           // i
    delete object_22;                                         // o
  }
  S *object_23 = nullptr;
  static S object_24("n", "h");                               // n
  S object_25("a", "c");                                      // a
  delete new S("l", "_");                                     // l
                                                              // _
  S *object_27 = new S("a", "g");                             // a
  S *object_28 = nullptr;
}                                                             // c
                                                              // c

// Main Thread Exit
// e
// s
// s
// :
// :
// w

// Program Exit
// h
// a
// t

// Answer: return value of bad_optional_access::what
```

Solution 128

```
void run() {
  delete new S("e", "f");                                     // e
                                                              // f
  thread_local S object_2("f", " ");                          // f
  new S("e", "x");                                            // e
  S object_4("c", "t");                                       // c
  static S object_5("t", "8");                                // t
  S *object_6 = nullptr;
  S *object_7 = new S(" ", "c");                              //
  object_6 = new S("o", "g");                                 // o
  S *object_8 = nullptr;
  S object_9("f", "i");                                       // f
```

```
{
  static S object_10(" ", "2");                    //
}
delete object_7;                                   // c
thread_local S object_11("a", "n");                // a
{
  S object_12("l", "w");                           // l
  {
    S *object_13 = nullptr;
    S object_14("l", "n");                         // l
    {
      object_8 = new S("i", "e");                  // i
      thread_local S object_15("n", " ");          // n
    }
    static S object_16("g", "1");                  // g
    {
      static S object_17(" ", " ");                //
      S object_18("L", "u");                       // L
      static S object_19("a", "=");                // a
      delete object_6;                             // g
    }                                              // u
    delete object_8;                               // e
    S object_20("r", "y");                         // r
    object_13 = new S("r", "k");                   // r
    S object_21("e", "l");                         // e
    S(" ", "p");                                   //
                                                   // p
    thread_local S object_23("o", "h");            // o
  }                                                // l
                                                   // y
                                                   // n
  {
    S object_24("o", " ");                         // o
    {
      S *object_25 = nullptr;
      {
        delete new S("m", "i");                    // m
                                                   // i
        static S object_27("a", ">");              // a
        S *object_28 = nullptr;
      }
      new S("l", "o");                             // l
    }
```

```
      S *object_30 = new S("s", "o");                   // s
    }                                                   //
  }                                                     // w
}                                                       // i
                                                        // t

// Main Thread Exit
// h
//
// n
//

// Program Exit
// >
// =
//
// 1
// 2
// 8

// Answer: effect of calling Laguerre polynomials with n >= 128
```

www.ingramcontent.com/pod-product-compliance
Lightning Source LLC
LaVergne TN
LVHW082245150826
845677LV00009B/1528

* 9 7 9 8 8 1 7 2 6 5 6 0 6 *